The Gift

Unfolding the Hidden Wisdom of Your Anxiety

Tabatha Kattau

Foreword

It is an absolute pleasure to introduce you to the work of my friend and colleague, Tabatha. In all my years of coaching, training, and mentoring individuals committed to self-awareness and transformation, Tabatha stands out as someone truly special. She approaches her work with a rare blend of insight, compassion, and dedication, creating a safe and supportive environment for anyone seeking to journey through the complexities of anxiety and uncover new ways of being.

Tabatha's passion for helping others goes beyond mere words. She is a natural empath with a gift for connecting deeply with people. Her life's mission—to guide others through their inner worlds with kindness and clarity—resonates in every chapter of this book. Her wisdom stems not only from her professional training but also from her own courageous journey of self-discovery. She knows firsthand what it means to navigate difficult emotions, to face fears, and to emerge with a renewed sense of strength and purpose. It's this authenticity that sets her apart and makes her guidance so incredibly impactful.

In this book, Tabatha has woven together practical tools with a rich understanding of the mind, body, and spirit, creating a resource that speaks directly to the heart of anyone struggling with anxiety or self-doubt. She offers a gentle yet powerful roadmap to uncovering the hidden wisdom within ourselves. Through thoughtful exercises, insightful stories, and compassionate reflections, Tabatha invites readers to see their anxiety not as an enemy but as a messenger—one that, when understood, can reveal pathways to resilience, peace, and self-acceptance.

As her trainer and supervisor, I have watched Tabatha flourish in her work and witnessed the many lives she has touched. I am consistently inspired by her commitment to learning, her openness to growth, and her unwavering dedication to supporting others. She has a way of seeing the potential in everyone, of reminding them that they are not broken but whole, that their anxieties and fears are not flaws but parts of a greater journey toward wholeness.

In reading this book, you'll experience the profound impact of Tabatha's insights and discover her heart-centred approach to healing and transformation. She brings a fresh perspective on anxiety, encouraging readers to view it as an invitation to grow rather than something to fear or resist. Her guidance is a reminder that within each of us lies the strength to overcome, redefine ourselves, and live a life rooted in authenticity and calm.

It is an honour to have Tabatha as a friend, and I am grateful to introduce you to her work, which I believe will resonate with anyone ready to transform their relationship with anxiety and reclaim a sense of peace. This book is not just a guide; it's a companion for anyone on the path to self-discovery and empowerment. Tabatha's words carry the warmth and sincerity of someone who truly understands and cares, and I trust that her wisdom will be as meaningful to you as it has been to so many others.

As you turn these pages, know that you are in safe and capable hands. This book is Tabatha's gift to you—a heartfelt offering from a woman with a heart of gold and an unwavering commitment to making the world a better place, one life at a time.

Dr. Heidi Heron PsyD
International NLP Master Trainer, Master Certified Coach

Dedication

I dedicate this book to my beautiful mum, Aleathea May Jemesen (1921–2010). Some may call her my foster mum, but to me, she is and always will be my true mother. She opened not only her home but her entire heart to me, filling my life with a love so profound that it continues to shape who I am and everything I do. Though she now watches over me from heaven, I feel her presence every day, guiding me with the same quiet strength and warmth she shared in life. As Maya Angelou once said, "People will forget what you said, they will forget what you did, but they will never forget how you made them feel." That is my mum's lasting gift to me. I will carry her love, her legacy, in my heart forever.

Dedication

Acknowledgments

To my family, thank you for your patience as I droned on about the book and how long it was taking and for all the countless hours you went without me while I tapped away endlessly on the front verandah. Your unwavering patience and support, as I gave up and started again many times, meant the world to me.

To my sisters and extended family—your love and acceptance have always been the wind beneath my wings. Thank you for everything.

I also want to express my gratitude to my biological mum, Lee. Without her difficult decision to entrust me into the care of another at such a young age, I wouldn't have become the woman I am today. She has taught me the incredible power of forgiveness, and for that, I am forever thankful.

A special thank you to my very first NLP coach, Sandip Mukherjee, who inspired me to start writing and encouraged me when I was full of self-doubt about what my words could offer. The book has certainly evolved from those early conversations, but I will always be grateful for his belief in me.

Thank you to Erin Lund, who helped me come up with the title of this book and reassured me that it was valid, soulful, and meaningful. Her belief in this book's potential to inspire and help others has been a guiding light.

My deep thanks to Robert Bruce and Mackayla Chalmers from the Enneagram Academy. Their compassionate inquiry methods and sacred space allowed me to unpack and understand the humble beginnings of my anxiety. I am forever grateful for their guidance and the space they held for me to learn to sit with my discomfort and find my own ways to navigate out of it.

To my incredible NLP Family, especially Dr. Heidi Heron—mentor, educator, coach, and friend. Words alone cannot express the love and gratitude I have for this remarkable human. Her generosity in sharing her wisdom has been beyond compare. I also want to thank her mother and business partner, Laureli Blyth, whose expertise in Advanced Hypnosis and Numerology took my understanding of NLP to another level.

To my friend and coach, Abi Hughes—until I met Abi, I never knew kindness could be both gentle and firm at the same time. She had my back when I needed it most, and I will always remember her support.

To Ingrid Hurwitz, whose trauma-informed exploration of the Enneagram helped me deepen my understanding of how childhood experiences shape our responses. Her loving, gentle enquiry methods enabled me to better understand myself and fuelled my courage to share my stories.

For my clients, who kept asking me how the book was going, sharing how eager they were to read it, and telling me who they were thinking of purchasing it for—I am deeply touched by your belief in me and this book. I hope it finds its way quickly into the hands of those who need it most, who you care for and want to help.

For my friends who cheered me on and remained excited and enthusiastic about this book, your energy and anticipation kept me typing on the hardest days. Your support means more than you know.

A huge thank you to Maisie, my trusty little canine companion, who sat beside me through countless writing sessions, offering quiet comfort and unconditional love.

To the unnamed woman who gave me Louise Hay's *You Can Heal Your Life*, you were the spark of inspiration for my book. You set me on this path, and I am forever grateful. I respect your need for anonymity, but please know that your generosity and gentle nature were constantly in my thoughts as I moved through this creative project.

To Louise Hay—your work ignited something in me that brought light to my darkest times and inspired me to go forth and bring relief and healing to others. Your legacy lives on in this book and the work I do.

To the amazing James Lee, my editor, who took my rugged first-ever manuscript and turned it into the incredible piece of work you are about to experience. I will be forever grateful for your knowledge, care, and expertise in making my dream of bringing support and relief from anxiety to the world… a reality. I also thank James for helping me realise I could publish the book myself.

And, of course, to the **readers** and **receivers** of this book—thank you for your trust. I hope it brings you the healing and wisdom you seek.

Finally, I want to acknowledge myself—just as I want the readers to acknowledge themselves. I know my mum would be so proud of me, and I am proud of myself, too. This journey has been one of growth, learning, and healing, and I hope this book inspires the same for everyone who reads it.

Contents

Introduction

Prologue

When I first thought about writing this book, I pictured it reaching out to people who felt lost and alone, just as I once did. I know that feeling well—the struggle to look composed on the outside while feeling broken and ashamed on the inside. I wanted to write a book that would leap off the shelf, calling, "Pick me up! I can help you!" But honestly, I wasn't sure how to make that happen.

The truth is, in my darkest hours, wisdom came to me as a gift. I was at a low point, weighed down by shame and guilt, unable to see a way forward. Then, one day, a dear friend passed by my desk, set down a small package, and simply said, "Here. This once helped me." And just like that, she was gone, and that moment shifted something in me. I pulled the package close and saw it contained a book and DVD called *You Can Heal Your Life* by Louise L. Hay. I paused. I'd tried counselling; I'd talked to friends and family, but nothing seemed to lift the darkness. Yet, something in her gesture stirred my curiosity. After all, what did I have to lose?

I'd lost so much weight. My smile had become rare, my steps were heavy, and each day, I dragged myself through the hours, just waiting for nightfall so I could take something to quiet my racing mind. But that afternoon, I felt the faintest flicker of hope—a subtle anticipation. I left work early and hurried home to an empty house, eager to watch the DVD. From the very first scene, I saw myself. My story was unique, yes, but the themes were all too familiar. I felt the same pain, the same searching, the same yearning for relief. And then the tears came—tears from a place I'd nearly forgotten, a place that held a small, rekindled hope that maybe, just maybe, life didn't have to be an endless struggle.

When the DVD ended, I looked over at the book lying beside me. It felt as if it were calling to me, waiting to be opened. But I had to pick up my kids from school, so I slipped the book into my bag and left. That drive felt different. The world seemed just a bit lighter, and it was comforting to know that book was with me, close by. Traveling with me. Like a quiet companion, it made me feel just a little less alone. "Who was this Louise Hay?" I wondered as I drove.

After those first few pages of *You Can Heal Your Life,* I was hooked. I went to every bookstore I could find, buying every Louise Hay book, calendar, audiobook, and meditation. I devoured her teachings because they made me feel better about myself. Her words were changing my life.

This is what I wanted for my own book—to reach those who feel unreachable, the ones who've tried everything and are close to giving up. But the more I thought about it, the more I realised something profound: I didn't find that book. It found me through someone who gifted it to me. And that gift began a journey to find the beautiful soul who had passed it along. Where was she now? How had this book found its way to her? I searched online and asked friends and colleagues, but there were no answers.

And then I stopped and thought—maybe it wasn't about finding her at all. Perhaps it was about something much more powerful—continuing the circle she had started. Her gift set something in motion, and perhaps my role was simply to keep that light moving forward. Who knows? Maybe, just as this book has now found its way to you, she might one day find her way back to me. But until then, I trust in the beautiful flow of this gifting circle—one that brings hope and healing to those who need it most. Like you.

A Book for Every Journey

If you're reading this book, you likely fall into one of three groups:

- **The Giver** – You bought this book for someone you care about, hoping to support them in their journey.

- **The Receiver** – Someone has gifted or loaned you this book with love and care.

- **The Self-Gifter** – You found this book in a store, and maybe, just maybe, it found you right back.

You know which one you are. Choose the message of gratitude below that speaks to you, and know that whatever brought this book into your hands, you're now part of a chain of compassion and healing.

A Message to the Giver

If you've watched a loved one struggle with anxiety and chose this book to help them, thank you. Your compassion and care matter more than you may know. Gestures like yours make a difference—not just to the person receiving this book but also to everyone touched by their healing. I remember a dear friend gifting me a book at a time when I felt lost and hopeless. She quietly placed it on my desk and said, "Here. This once helped me." That simple gesture changed the course of my life. And now, your gift has the potential to bring healing to someone you care about deeply.

It can be hard to know how to support someone with anxiety. You might feel the urge to fix things or say the "right" words, but sometimes the most profound support comes from simply being there—without judgment, without rushing. Ask them how you can help, respect their space, and honour your own boundaries. Healing takes time, and your loved one may not always be ready to talk or engage. Remember, their journey to healing is uniquely theirs, and your role is to be a steady, loving presence alongside them.

As you walk this path with them, consider reciting this affirmation each morning:

"Today, I send healing blessings to the person I gifted this book. With every word they read, they grow, heal, and find peace. My love and compassion reach far beyond this moment, offering light to all who need it. My kindness ripples out, expanding joy, understanding, and support."

This is your daily reminder that your kindness carries energy beyond what you can see. Take a moment each morning to send love to your recipient and feel your own heart expand as you witness the power of your gift.

A Message to the Receiver

This book has found its way to you because someone deeply cares about your well-being. I know how it feels to be overwhelmed—to feel like your mind is racing and there's no way out. I've been there too. In my darkest times, it felt like my anxiety was a black hole, swallowing any glimmer of hope. But a small gift—a book and DVD from a friend—sparked something inside me. I remember sitting alone, letting the words and stories wash over me, and, for the first time in a long time, I felt a flicker of hope. This moment will pass, and you are stronger than you know.

All I ask is that you keep this book close. Slip it into your bag, let it be by your side, and hold it to your heart when things feel heavy. Glance at it once a day, even if only for a moment. And when you need an anchor, speak this affirmation:

"I am worthy of love, support, and peace. With each breath, I release a bit more of my pain, and with each page, I welcome a little more hope. I trust that this journey will unfold just as I need it to, and I open myself to receive all the love and healing that surrounds me. I am never alone, and each day brings me closer to my calm, true self."

Let these words be a touchstone. As you wake up each day, repeat this affirmation, feeling the strength of your worth and the hope that grows with every breath. You are on a path to healing, and this affirmation will remind you to welcome all the support, love, and peace that comes your way.

A Message to the Self-Gifter

To the person who picked up this book for themselves: I want to acknowledge the courage it took to reach for help. In a world that often tells us to "push through" or "get over it," seeking support can feel like a radical act of self-love. I remember the first time I bought a book to help me navigate my anxiety. It felt almost like finding a secret key to a door I didn't know existed—a door to a deeper understanding of myself and to tools that helped me begin to heal. Just as that book became a companion to me, I hope this one becomes a safe space for you.

Make time each day to read, even if it's just for a few minutes. Protect that time as a small ritual for yourself. And, as you start your day, begin with this affirmation:

"By choosing this book, I have chosen myself. Each day, I dedicate time to healing, to understanding, and to growing. I trust in my ability to reclaim my peace and joy, knowing that my commitment to myself is an act of deep love and courage. I am ready to embrace the power within me, step by step, word by word."

Every morning, as you say this affirmation, let it remind you of your commitment to yourself. This is a journey of reclaiming your peace, and each word you speak is a step closer to your inner calm. Know that you are brave, you are loved, and you are worthy of all the healing you seek.

Preparing to Read This Book

Welcome to a path of self-discovery and healing. This book is designed to feel like a private therapy session, but one where you are both the therapist and the client, gently guiding yourself toward new insights and understanding. Throughout these pages, you'll encounter questions that invite reflection, stories that may stir emotions or memories, and exercises that encourage you to think in new, empowering ways. At times, you may feel challenged by ideas or perspectives that feel unfamiliar. Embrace these moments as part of the process and approach each one with an open heart and mind. *What are you hoping to gain here? Set your intention, and trust that whatever you need will reveal itself as you read.*

This book is a space for safety and growth, much like being in my virtual or physical therapy room, free from blame or judgment. I understand that you are doing the best you can with the knowledge and resources you have right now. My aim isn't to tell you how you "should" be feeling or living; rather, it's to offer you new perspectives, insights, and tools to help you navigate anxiety and embrace a deeper sense of peace. In the spirit of neuro-linguistic programming (NLP), the foundational approach woven throughout this book, we believe that when you know better, you can do better. This book is your invitation to know better—in a loving, gentle way.

As you move through these pages, things will begin to shift for you—in supportive, helpful ways. You may start to notice changes in how you see yourself, your thoughts, and your experiences. Even now, as you prepare to start reading, you may sense that a new possibility is beginning to unfold for you. That's right.

How to Make the Most of This Book

I suggest grabbing a notepad or journal that's yours exclusively for this experience. Use it as a safe space to jot down thoughts, reflect on the exercises, and capture anything meaningful that comes up as you read. If writing isn't your style, consider drawing, doodling, or simply sitting quietly with the material, letting it sink in. There's no "right" way to engage, only what feels most meaningful to you.

Find a quiet, comfortable place to read. Maybe it's a cozy chair at home or perhaps a quiet nook outdoors where you feel most at ease. Bring a cup of tea, coffee, or whatever brings you joy, and allow yourself to settle into this moment. This is your time, your space to grow and heal. You can take breaks, revisit chapters, and move at a pace that feels right for you. And remember, this is a safe space; you're in control of how deeply you choose to engage with each part of this experience.

What Lies Ahead

This book is designed to feel like a gentle conversation with your inner self, guiding you toward new perspectives and skills. As you read, here's what you'll find:

- **Understanding Anxiety:** You'll uncover the true effects of anxiety, seeing how it impacts not only your thoughts but also your body, relationships, and daily experiences. You'll discover safe, practical ways to release pent-up emotions and uncover the hidden stories that may be fueling anxious thoughts.

- **Changing Your Patterns:** Through hands-on exercises, you'll explore ways to separate beliefs from behaviours, spot hidden influences, and reshape your thoughts to build a more empowering story for yourself. Some of the ideas might be new, but each is here with the purpose of helping you make meaningful changes.

- **Connecting Mind and Body:** You'll learn how your mind works and see how neuro-linguistic programming (NLP) can support you in processing experiences. You'll explore how closely your thoughts and physical well-being are linked. This section may lead you to question some beliefs or patterns but keep in mind— that growth often comes from gently stepping outside familiar habits.

- **Creating Your Future Self:** Through practising visualisation and grounding, you'll shape a clear picture of the person you want to become. Practical steps and reflections will help you make this vision real, allowing you to create a more peaceful relationship with yourself beyond anxiety.

Prepare for an experience that will unfold step by step, inviting fresh insights, meaningful choices, and real growth. I'm honored to be by your side as you work through this book. *Are you ready to begin?* Let's get started.

CHAPTER 1

Understanding Anxiety's Impact

"What we think about ourselves becomes the truth for us."

~ Louise L. Hay

Anxiety can be hard to spot from the outside, but its effects run deep. Often, it isn't just about feeling nervous or overwhelmed—it's a quiet force that subtly reshapes our lives, narrowing our worlds little by little. You might find yourself avoiding situations or turning down opportunities, making choices that seem easier in the moment but slowly erode your confidence, your connections, and even your sense of self.

In this chapter, we'll look at the ways anxiety can impact every corner of life—from our relationships and social circles to our health and happiness. It's easy to think that avoiding certain triggers is a solution, yet in reality, these choices can lead us further away from the life we want. Together, we'll explore what these hidden costs look like and reflect on what it means to start reclaiming control from anxiety's hold.

To begin, I want to share a story that captures the moment I realised something was off in my own life. It was a quiet moment, one I might have brushed off—but instead, it became a starting point for recognising the invisible power anxiety had over me.

My Story - *The Night I Knew Something Wasn't Quite Right*

I still vividly recall that cold winter evening, sitting frozen in the car while my friends gathered around a campfire. Their laughter echoed through the darkness as they shared stories and toasted marshmallows. My boyfriend kept coming back to the car, coaxing me to join them. Each time he returned, his frustration grew.

Why wouldn't I come out? Why was I just sitting there, unmoving? I kept insisting it was warmer in the car—after all, we were near the

Barrington Tops, where it often snowed—but deep down, I knew warmth wasn't the reason I was staying put.

Inside, my body felt paralysed. I urged myself to open the door and go and laugh with my friends.

But something inside me refused to move. I could hear their voices, their joyful chatter, and I felt a knot of shame and confusion tightening in my chest. How I wished I could just start the car and drive—drive anywhere, away from this scene and, more importantly, away from this feeling.

My thoughts began to race. How could they be so happy? Many of my friends didn't have the well-paying job I had, the car, or the close-knit family. And yet they were carefree, laughing and smiling. Why couldn't I share in their joy? What was wrong with me? The anxiety only deepened as my mind sped up. Was I losing my mind? Was this the start of a nervous breakdown? But why? What did I even have to feel nervous about?

I had no idea that this would be just the first of many frantic episodes— moments of questioning, worrying, and wanting to escape my own body. It would take me years to understand that this was a panic attack.

That night, as I sat frozen in my car, I made a decision: camping trips just weren't for me. But it wasn't the camping that had caused my anxiety. It was something deeper, something unseen that I couldn't quite put my finger on. So, instead of addressing the source of my anxiety, I began to avoid the things that seemed to trigger it. Promotions, social events, public speaking opportunities, mother's groups, hobbies... even birthday parties and weddings. Difficult conversations and setting boundaries felt impossible. Slowly, I withdrew from life, mistaking these external experiences for the cause of my internal turmoil.

Have you ever found yourself avoiding situations, convinced it would make things easier?

What I didn't realise then was that it wasn't these activities I needed to remove—it was the anxiety itself. These were the unseen, true costs of anxiety, silently chipping away at my world.

The True Costs of an Anxious Mind

So, what about you? As you read my story, perhaps you found pieces of yourself reflected in those moments of fear and self-doubt—moments when your anxiety kept you frozen in place, feeling cut off from joy, connection, or the life you truly wanted to live. Just as I sat there in the car, desperately trying to will myself into the world of laughter and warmth, you might recognise the ways anxiety has limited your choices or led you to withdraw.

What has anxiety cost you? Your freedom, peace, or sense of calm? Confidence, safety, or security? Maybe, like me, you've found yourself removing things from your life—one by one—in an attempt to sidestep the anxiety. Relationships, opportunities, hobbies, or experiences that once brought you joy are now sacrificed, all in the name of "avoiding" that dreadful feeling.

But what if these weren't just isolated choices? What if they were building blocks of an unseen, growing pattern that has quietly shaped the way you live?

Take a moment to consider: What are some of the things you've systematically let go of, convinced that these changes would "solve" the anxiety? Consider jotting down a few examples in your notebook or journal. This will help you explore patterns over time. And how much have those sacrifices really cost you?

The Impact of Chronic Anxiety

Anxiety isn't just feeling a bit worried or stressed—it's a deeper, more unsettling experience. It's that sensation of fear or unease gripping you, even when there's no real danger. It's your nervous system sounding the alarm when things only seem threatening, even if they're not as dangerous as they feel.

If that sounds familiar, know that you're not alone. Around 275 million people worldwide live with anxiety, including 3.4 million in Australia alone. That's a lot of people—people just like you and me— doing their best to navigate life while carrying that heavy, anxious weight. It's something that affects not just our emotions but also our relationships, our work, and even our physical health. And let's not forget the financial cost—trillions of dollars spent globally on doctors, hospitals, medications, and lost productivity.

In Australia alone, anxiety and other mental health struggles come with a staggering price tag of about 28.6 billion Australian dollars every year. This isn't just the cost of treatment; it's the cost of people missing work, opportunities slipping by, and lives being impacted in countless ways.

But let's put the statistics aside for a moment. This isn't just about numbers—it's about real lives, like yours and mine. I felt compelled to write this book because I've been there, and I understand how isolating and overwhelming it can feel. My goal is to offer support, a hand to hold, as you navigate your anxiety and come to see that you are not alone on this journey.

So, let's bring it back to you. If you have a notebook or journal nearby, take it out and let these questions be an invitation to explore:

- *What do you notice about how anxiety shows up in your life?*

- *Where do you feel it most—physically, emotionally, financially?*
- *What do you believe it costs your relationships, your work, your sense of peace?*

As you write, be gentle with yourself. This isn't about finding answers right away but about beginning to explore what lies beneath the surface.

The Impact on You

In my deepest moments of anxiety, I felt paralysed by fear. My stomach would twist, my heart would race, and my mind would frantically search for the cause of my distress. To me, anxiety felt like the herald of something bad—a shadowy threat just out of sight. I couldn't tell you what that "bad" thing was, but I felt its presence, a constant unease simmering beneath the surface. That's what anxiety meant to me. But we each have our own meaning, our own experience.

Take a moment now and reflect: What does anxiety mean to you? As you think about this, consider how your body responds when anxiety shows up.

For many of us, anxiety feels like an alarm system that never quite shuts off. The neurons in your brain start firing at the slightest hint of a threat, trying to predict, prepare for, or avoid any possible harm. And then the thoughts begin—racing through all the potential "what ifs," scanning for the worst-case scenarios. With this whirlwind of thoughts, your body often follows suit.

Maybe you notice a tightening in your shoulders, your jaw, or your chest. Perhaps your breath becomes shallow, like there's a knot tied somewhere in your lungs that makes it hard to exhale fully. And as the fear surges, so does the adrenaline—flooding your system, speeding up your heartbeat, and leaving your stomach to churn with unease, possibly sending you to the bathroom as your body struggles to make sense of it all.

Anxiety lives not just in your mind, but in your entire being—your head, your heart, and your gut. And over the years, this constant state of high alert can take a toll, leaving you feeling worn down, exhausted, and perhaps even disconnected from yourself. Anxiety asks so much of you, and it's no wonder that your body, heart, and mind feel weary from carrying the load.

But I want you to pause here and recognise something important: You have carried all of this because, at some level, your body believed it needed to protect you. Every tight muscle, every racing thought, every flutter in your gut—they were all ways your body tried to keep you safe. And while anxiety may have worn you down, let's take a moment to thank your body for all it has done and for all the times it held you together when you felt like you were falling apart. Thank your heart for beating strong, even when it felt heavy. Thank your mind for its determination to find answers, even when those answers weren't clear.

You and your body deserve better than this constant battle. And I want you to know that change is possible. It's possible to release that burden, find a safe harbour, and step into a life where anxiety no longer runs the show. As you read on, may you find the tools, the relief, and the hope to let go of the battle—bit by bit—and finally come back to yourself.

Exhale and acknowledge the impact anxiety has had on you. This is where your path to healing begins.

The Impact on Your Family & Friends

When anxiety takes over, it's normal to want to withdraw from socialising—even with those closest to you. Have you ever felt like the thought of facing a room full of people, even your own family, was just too much? Perhaps you've declined an invitation, made an excuse, or cancelled plans at the last minute because the idea of being around others felt overwhelming. When anxiety is present, even being with the people we love can seem daunting.

Maybe you know this feeling all too well—the sense that you're carrying something you can't quite share. You might feel like you're living a double life, pretending to be okay when underneath, the anxiety feels like it's simmering just below the surface.

Have you ever caught yourself wondering, *Do you fear what might happen if your anxiety suddenly kicks in while you're with your family or friends?*

Or perhaps you've thought, *How will you make a quick escape without drawing attention to yourself? And what if they see—truly see— that you're struggling?*

Anxiety often has a way of making you feel like a burden to those around you. Like it's something they need to fix, or worse, something they pity. Do you secretly wonder if your family and friends get tired of hearing about your struggles? If they're fed up with trying to help? If they're just pretending to understand, when in truth, they may not know how to reach you.

Maybe these fears lead you to withdraw even more, keeping a distance to avoid feeling like you're "too much" for them to handle. Or perhaps you don't share what's really going on in your mind because, deep down, you worry they might think you're "crazy." And that thought is just too much to bear.

But what does this mean for your relationships? It means missing out on deep, meaningful connections. It means feeling like you're watching life from behind a foggy window, unable to reach out and truly touch the world around you. And maybe, somewhere along the way, you've convinced yourself that you're fine with that. But ask yourself: Is that really your heart talking? Or is it your anxiety?

For me, anxiety often meant missing out on moments that mattered. I remember when I declined an invitation to my closest friend's wedding. I just didn't have the mental energy to manage all the details—organising the family, finding care for the kids, asking my husband to rearrange his plans. Each small task felt like a mountain to climb, and in the end, I chose what felt like the easier path: not going at all. But while I avoided the anxiety of attending, I couldn't avoid the pain of hurting my friend or the hurt I felt myself for not being there. When you live with anxiety, every decision feels like choosing which pain is easier to bear.

What about you? Have there been moments like this for you, too? Times when your anxiety held you back from fully being there with the people who matter most? It's not just you who misses out—your friends and family miss out on the real you, the version of you that is more than the anxiety that covers it.

But I know that you don't need me to tell you what you're missing out on. Deep down, you already know. And it hurts. It hurts to feel so hopeless, to wonder if things will ever change. But here's something important: You're here. You're reading these words, seeking to understand yourself and find a way forward. And that is no small step. You've already taken a leap toward changing how anxiety impacts not just you, but your relationships as well.

And for that, I am proud of you. Because healing is a journey, and you're already on the path.

The Impact on Your Community

I'm an introvert. It's not that I don't like people—I do. I just prefer my own company most of the time. I enjoy my thoughts, and I'm drawn to activities that let me explore my inner world. For me, this is a choice I make intentionally.

But that wasn't always the case. When I was in the grip of chronic anxiety, my thoughts weren't a place of comfort—they were a place of fear. A scary, unsettling place that I tried to avoid at all costs. So, I kept myself busy. I worked hard, organised the family, and longed for the moment night would fall so I could take medication, numb my mind, and finally fall asleep.

Back then, the idea of "community" was foreign to me. I felt alone, and the very thought of engaging in a community felt like another burden—a need I couldn't fulfil. I had nothing left to give, and the anxiety made sure of that. It pushed me to withdraw from social situations, and over time, I isolated myself more and more, sinking deeper into loneliness. I wasn't part of any kind of community. I didn't see myself as someone who had a role or a presence in the place where I lived. I was just trying to survive.

Maybe this feels familiar to you—the sense that being part of a community is something you simply can't handle right now. That if you engage, you'll be expected to do something, give something, or, worse, find a way to eventually get out of it when it becomes too much. Anxiety convinces you it's easier to stay on the outside, to keep a distance. But what does that cost you? And what does it cost your community?

Take a moment to reflect: Where are you in your community? What comes up when you think about the people who live around you, work with you, or share similar interests with you? What do you notice about how anxiety holds you back from being part of these circles?

For years, I didn't realise the impact this disconnection had on my life. But once I started to overcome my anxiety, I began to see things differently. I started taking long walks around my town, enjoying the beautiful areas and saying "hi" to familiar faces. I even found that sometimes my neighbour and I would be out walking our dogs at the same time, and we'd end up strolling together, side by side. It felt... nice. Easy. And something shifted within me—this simple connection made me feel like I belonged. And belonging brought a sense of safety, a feeling of being rooted.

One of the most eye-opening moments for me was when my region experienced significant flooding a couple of years ago. Homes were lost, lives were turned upside down, and the crisis centres were overwhelmed with people in need of support. Without hesitation, I jumped into my car and drove to one of these centres to offer my therapy services. At first, they turned me away, saying they had enough help. And, to be honest, the old me would have taken that as a sign to go home, to reinforce the story of not being needed, not being worthy. But something had changed in me—I wasn't led by anxiety anymore.

When they called me back, asking if I could return because they did, in fact, need my help, I went. I stayed for three days, offering whatever support I could to those in distress. And what I found was that being part of my community in that moment—standing with them in their pain and recovery—was one of the most humbling and powerful experiences of my life. I would have missed that. I would have missed connecting with people in such a profound way—if anxiety had still been my guide.

I've also learned that "community" doesn't have to mean 'where you live.' For me, my strongest sense of community is with my NLP family from the NLP Worldwide Institute. Community is not just about geography—it's about finding a group of people who share a common bond, a shared experience. And perhaps that's true for you, too. A community can be a church group, a circle of friends, an online space, or even a professional network. But wherever it is, know that when anxiety is impacting your life, your community is missing out on you: the real you, the one who is more than anxiety.

When I let go of my chronic anxiety, my beliefs about community changed. I began to trust that my community valued me—not for what I could do for them, but for who I was. They valued my work, my presence, and my story. And yes, there are probably still some people in my community who find me a bit annoying, but that's okay. I know who I am now. I am not my anxiety, and neither are you.

As you read this, I want you to start to imagine what it would be like to reconnect with your community—not as someone who needs to be "fixed," but as someone who has something to offer. You might be surprised at how much they welcome you in. And more than that, you might be surprised at how much you have to give and how much of a difference your presence can make. Because when you step out of the shadows of anxiety, you step into the truth of who you really are. And that truth is your strength; it's your passport back to living fully and feeling like you truly belong.

The Impact on the World

When I was in the grip of anxiety, my world got small. Really small. I retracted, hid away, and avoided anything that might bring on more of those unsettling feelings. I stopped watching the news (a choice I still stand by), stopped going to events, and even found grocery shopping almost unbearable. I severed my ties with society, convinced that if I just stayed in my bubble, I could stay safe.

But let's pause and think about that. How does withdrawing like this impact the world? Maybe right now, you're thinking, "The world's got billions of people—it won't notice if I don't participate." But I want to challenge that. Yes, the world is vast, and yes, there are many people. But here's the thing: None of them are you. None of them think, feel, or see the world in quite the way you do. And that's exactly why your presence matters.

The world needs people like you—people who feel deeply, who think in the depths of oceans rather than skimming the surface like raindrops on a puddle. The world needs people who understand the struggle, who have danced with despair, and who can bring that rare gift of empathy and understanding to those who are hurting. Anxiety may have kept you hidden, but it has also given you an immense capacity to connect with others on a level that is both profound and meaningful.

Take a moment to think about how much you may have shrunk your world to keep anxiety at bay. Perhaps, like me, you designed your life around avoiding any situation that might trigger discomfort. Did you find yourself weighing every choice with worst-case consequences? Maybe you dismissed dreams or ambitions—anything that could leave you vulnerable to criticism or embarrassment. If the answer was yes, then the response to opportunity was always no. And with every "no" came a tightening of possibilities, like closing off doors one by one until you found yourself living within the narrowest of rooms.

But I want to invite you to catch that dismissive tendency, the one that might already be popping up as you read this. To notice how anxiety has trained you to think smaller, safer, more contained thoughts in the name of security. And then I want to remind you of something powerful: You weren't born this way. There was a time—perhaps as a child—when you believed anything was possible when your dreams were as boundless as the sky. And here's the truth: That same boundlessness still lives within you.

Anxiety has its place, and I'm not here to shame or dismiss it. This whole journey is about befriending anxiety, learning to listen to its wisdom, and seeing how it's tried to protect you. But it's also about expanding your perspective—stretching your mind beyond the confines of anxiety and starting to imagine what might be possible for you again. It's about opening those doors you've closed and peeking into the world of potential that lies just beyond.

Because the world needs you in your fullness. Not necessarily as a movie star or a world-renowned author (though those dreams are welcome too!)—but as you, offering whatever unique gifts and contributions only you can bring. The world is richer, more vibrant, and more complete when you show up...as YOU.

Reflective Exercise

1. Think about an area of life where anxiety has encouraged you to withdraw. What would it look like to slowly re-engage with that world?

2. Consider one small action you could take to reconnect with a community or group that once brought you joy or comfort. Imagine how it would feel to show up fully without the filter of anxiety.

3. Take a few deep breaths and envision the impact your presence

can make. What might you share with the world if you allowed yourself to step forward again?

Affirmation

"I am worthy of connection, and I have something valuable to offer the world. I embrace my unique presence and trust that I am needed."

CHAPTER 2

Releasing and Expressing Emotions

"The cave you fear to enter holds the treasure you seek."

~ Joseph Campbell

Before we dive into your specific anxiety, let's start by letting off some steam—getting what's inside... outside. Think of it like when your handbag gets too full. You notice it's heavier, and suddenly, it's hard to find what you need. You know you need to clean it out, but you're unsure what to keep or toss. Day by day, the job feels bigger, and your bag only gets heavier and harder to carry around. Before you can lighten the load, you need to empty it first. You have to see what's inside weighing it down. Only then can you decide what to keep, what no longer serves you, and what to let go of.

Emotions work the same way. Holding everything inside takes energy. Some of what we carry was once useful; some have simply become heavy and unhelpful. When the weight gets too much to bear, finding safe ways to release it can make all the difference. Once we've let it out, we can start choosing what to hold onto and what to release.

There are many ways to let out what's building up inside, and I've tried almost all of them. In this chapter, I'll guide you through safe ways to release your emotions, helping you feel lighter, freer, and ready to move forward.

My Story - *Learning to Release*

When my mum passed away in 2010, I felt abandoned. Her love had been a kind of safe haven, a unique, unconditional warmth I didn't think I'd ever feel again. Losing her awakened my inner child, bringing back fears of being alone... again.

My foster mum had taken me in as a six-month-old baby when she was 52. Now, as I write this, I'm 51—a year younger than she was when she chose to foster me. I can't imagine the strength it took for her to raise me alone, but somehow, she did it with unwavering patience, compassion, and love.

I adored this woman. Losing her tore through me, a pain I felt deep in my core. Even surrounded by loved ones, I felt they couldn't truly understand my grief. How could they? How could they grasp the weight of feeling so deliberately, so completely chosen—only to have that love taken away?

The grief became overwhelming, and I knew I needed a way to process it. I needed to let it all out. So, one night, with my husband and children away, I ran a hot bath. I sat there, knees pulled close, letting the warmth surround me. And then, I cried. I cried like a child, letting every bit of sorrow surface. Soon, I was practically bathing in my own tears, my cries growing louder and louder until I was howling. Alone on our 30-acre property, I finally let myself feel it all, shouting, "No! No! No!" and pleading, "Don't leave me. Please don't leave me." I was like a heartbroken child begging to be held.

After several minutes, the intense ache loosened its grip. It was still there, but softer and smaller. This wasn't a pretty process, but it was real and a release. Not all of my methods have been this intense, but that one was necessary at the time.

Physical and Written Releases

When it comes to letting out pent-up emotions, there are several options—physical, verbal, and written—and the best approach depends on what feels right for you. Below are some safe methods to explore, each one allowing you to express what's inside in a way that feels manageable and authentic.

Sharing How You're Feeling

Talking with a trusted friend or family member can be a powerful way to release emotions, though it depends on how open you feel and whether that person can hold space without judgment. I remember trying to share my anxiety with those close to me, hoping to feel seen, heard, and understood. But I often feared burdening them, and my anxiety convinced me they wouldn't fully understand. Setting the tone up front can help, such as saying something like: "I just need you to listen. I'm not looking for advice. I just need to share what's on my mind. Is that okay?"

Sometimes, sharing brought instant relief; other times, well-meaning friends would try to "fix" my feelings, leaving me feeling misunderstood. It's not a perfect solution, but even a simple acknowledgment from a friend—"I hear you, and I'm here"—can make a big difference in feeling understood and less alone.

Speaking with a Professional

Therapists, counsellors, or psychologists can offer an objective space to release what's weighing you down. I didn't resonate with traditional counselling; I often felt judged and unsafe, likely due to the skill of the counsellor I saw. Looking back, I could have tried different counsellors, but my anxiety left me exhausted and too embarrassed to keep searching.

For me, NLP therapy was life-changing. It was the first time I felt truly safe, fully accepted, and understood. Instead of focusing on my mistakes, NLP helped me imagine goals and outcomes that felt achievable beyond my anxiety. Whether it's NLP or another type of therapy, finding a professional who feels right for you is key.

If you're not ready for therapy, consider starting with a conversation with your GP. It might feel intimidating, but speaking with a doctor can often be a first step toward finding the right support.

My Story - *Finding My Lifeline*

One night, during a peak moment of anxiety, I felt hopeless. I couldn't escape my ruminating thoughts…I was at my wits' end. I wouldn't say I was suicidal, but I felt trapped, convinced my life would be a never-ending stream of scary, worrying thoughts. I was exhausted and felt so alone. Even when I spoke with family, as well-meaning as they were, I didn't feel truly heard. Most told me, "You'll snap out of it," or "Don't worry so much; it will pass." Or, "Just pick yourself up."

Such well-intentioned advice, but I remember thinking, *Don't you think if people could snap out of it, they would? Do you think anyone would choose to live in constant fear and worry?*

One night, feeling completely overwhelmed, I snuck out of bed and stepped outside. Raising my phone in the dark, I called Lifeline. When the kind woman on the other end picked up, I immediately apologised. "I'm not suicidal," I reassured her, "and I'm so sorry for wasting your time. There's probably someone who needs this way more than me." Guilt washed over me as tears streamed down my face; I didn't even feel worthy of this small support. But she gently reassured me, speaking with me for the next 15 or 20 minutes, allowing me to pour out what had been trapped inside. By the end of the call, I felt calm enough to go back to bed and try to sleep.

When I hung up the phone, I looked up at the stars. For the first time in a long time, I didn't feel quite as alone. Thank you, Lifeline.

Movement and Sound Releases

Sometimes, words aren't enough—your body needs its own way to let go of what it's holding onto. Movement and sound can be incredibly effective for releasing pent-up anxiety.

Screaming or Punching into Pillows

Screaming, whether out loud or into a pillow, might seem a bit odd, but it's surprisingly effective for reducing tension and stress. Letting out a loud scream can activate your parasympathetic nervous system, which helps calm your body. I remember feeling a bit silly the first time I tried screaming into a pillow, but the relief was undeniable. It was like letting off the pressure from a boiling kettle. Find a private space and try it—you might feel silly, but you might also feel a weight lift from you. Really, what do you have to lose?

Dancing and Moving Your Body

When your mind feels stuck, movement can help shift that energy. Dancing to your favourite music, even if it's just a quick sway around your living room, lets you express emotions physically. You don't have to look graceful—the goal is to move freely and let the energy flow out. Personally, I struggled with dancing when anxiety was at its worst; joy felt unreachable. But I tried, and even if dancing didn't always shift my mood completely, just moving made a difference.

If thinking of it as "shaking off stress" rather than dancing helps, go for it. Put on a song and let your body take over.

Singing

Singing is another powerful way to let out emotion. Studies show that singing reduces stress and activates the vagus nerve, helping your body relax. For me, singing in the car became a cathartic release, letting me pour my emotions into the lyrics that resonated with me. It might not work for everyone, but it's worth trying—loudly or softly, whatever feels good to you. And if belting it out is your style, maybe try the back roads instead of your local town centre… but hey, whatever works!

Physical and Reflective Practices

These are gentler ways to connect with your body and quiet your mind, helping you release emotional tension.

Yoga

Yoga offers a variety of practices, from gentle Hatha to vigorous Vinyasa, each suited to different needs. Finding the right class makes all the difference. My first experience wasn't exactly smooth—I showed up to what I thought would be a gentle class, only to realise I was in an advanced session. Five minutes in, I felt like everyone was watching me struggle through poses that made me feel like a pretzel ready to snap. All I could think was, *What am I doing here? How can I leave without causing a scene?* Anxiety won that day; I stayed, painfully aware of how out of place I felt.

Eventually, I found a beautiful, gentle yoga class where the teacher encouraged me, "Do what you can, and that's enough." Yoga became one of my favorite tools for managing stress and anxiety. It reminded me that this journey isn't about perfection—it's about showing up and being present with what is.

Pilates

Don't be fooled by the gentle appearance of some Pilates instructors—mine looked as graceful as a ballerina but had the strength and discipline of a drill sergeant. She knew exactly how to work muscles I didn't even know existed. My first session left me so exhausted that I threw up, but it was also a powerful release.

Pilates wasn't gentle like yoga; it was tough. But it helped me reconnect with my body in a different way. The burn of the exercises grounded me, pulling me out of my anxious mind and into my physical body. Over time, I felt stronger and more confident in what my body could do. Pilates didn't provide the same sense of rest and reflection that yoga did, but it brought a new sense of strength and resilience.

Reflective Exercises: Try It Out

1. **Release through Sound or Movement:** Choose one of the methods above—screaming, dancing, or singing—and give it a try. Afterwards, reflect: *How did it feel to let go physically? Did it shift your mood or bring any relief?*

2. **Explore Physical Practices:** Consider trying a gentle yoga or Pilates class, even just a short session online. Reflect on how the movement makes you feel. Does it help you reconnect with your body or find a moment of calm?

3. **Personal Comfort Zone:** Identify any release methods that feel most approachable or challenging. What might make you more comfortable with trying them?

Gentle Everyday Releases

Sometimes, the most effective ways to release emotions are the simplest, requiring no planning or preparation.

Walking

Walking has to be my number one go-to for managing anxiety. There's something about putting one foot in front of the other, feeling the rhythm of your steps, and letting your thoughts wander that just… works.

Have you ever noticed that when people are faced with a problem, they often start pacing? That's because walking boosts creativity and helps with problem-solving. For me, walking feels like untangling the knots in my mind, and I often come up with ideas for therapy, social media posts, or even ways to take better care of myself. Sometimes, a simple walk is all it takes to feel back on track.

And it's not just me—Mark Zuckerberg and Steve Jobs were known to hold walking meetings. They tapped into the same benefits that walking offers all of us: clarity, focus, and a sense of calm through simple movement.

Meditation

I never realised how powerful meditation could be—or how little you actually need to make it work. When I first considered meditation, I found the idea terrifying. I was already trying hard to escape my thoughts, and suddenly, the suggestion was to sit with them. Facing the constant whirring of my mind felt like the last thing I wanted.

But the more I tried, the more I realised that meditation isn't about sitting alone with your thoughts. It's about *witnessing* them. That shift was a game-changer for me. Meditation allowed me to observe my thoughts without getting tangled up in them, like watching clouds drift across the sky without feeling the need to chase after them.

I started with guided meditations, and Louise Hay became my go-to. I must have listened to every recording she ever made. Having someone else's voice to guide me helped me relax and stay focused. If you're new to meditation, there are countless free options on YouTube. Just keep in mind that the choices can feel overwhelming, so it helps to set an intention first. Ask yourself: *What do I need from meditation right now?* Are you looking for calm, help falling asleep, or clarity on a difficult decision? Knowing your intention can help you find a meditation that aligns with what you need.

These days, I prefer a simpler approach. I sit, focus on my breathing—in for four counts, hold for four, out for four—and repeat until my body settles. Then I notice the sensations: where my body touches the chair, the texture of the ground under my feet. From there, I let my thoughts rise and fall, asking questions in my mind and letting whatever comes up simply exist. Sometimes, I set a timer; other times, I trust my intuition to know when I'm finished.

For me, meditation is a way to witness and release thoughts. It's especially effective when paired with other releases, like walking or dancing. Think of meditation as a practice of returning to yourself, giving your mind permission to slow down and just *be*.

Reflective Exercises: Gentle Releases

1. **Walk with Intention:** Next time you go for a walk, try going without music or distractions. Focus on the rhythm of your steps and notice what thoughts come up. How does your mind feel after 10–15 minutes of walking? Jot down any new insights or ideas afterwards.

2. **Beginner's Meditation:** If you're new to meditation, start with a guided session online. Reflect afterwards: *How did it feel to simply observe your thoughts? Did it bring a sense of calm or clarity?*

3. **Set a Meditation Intention**: Before your next meditation, set an intention based on what you're seeking. Whether it's relaxation, insight, or emotional release, notice how having an intention shapes your experience.

Final Thoughts on Releasing Emotions

How are you feeling after exploring these different ways to let out what's been pent up inside? Maybe one or two approaches resonate more strongly, or perhaps you have other strategies of your own that help you release what you're carrying. And that's the beauty of this journey—it's not about doing things perfectly; it's about trying different approaches, discovering what feels right, and knowing that every step you take is progress.

Remember, the goal is to gently release the emotional weight you've been holding, creating space for new perspectives and possibilities. Each practice helps you find your own unique way to let go, breathe, and begin moving toward a place of freedom and calm. This journey might be messy, imperfect, and sometimes even uncomfortable. And that's okay.

So, as you consider ways to release your emotions, be gentle with yourself, celebrate each step forward, and know that real strength lies in showing up—whatever that looks like for you.

CHAPTER 3

Unhealthy Coping Mechanisms

"Ask not why the addiction, but why the pain."

~ Gabor Mate

In the last chapter, we explored safe, healthy ways to release the emotions and anxiety you've been holding inside. But there's another side to letting go of what we carry—a side I know too well. These are ways of releasing emotions that can feel like relief in the moment but often come with consequences that hurt us even more.

Not-so-Safe Ways of Releasing Emotions

If you find yourself using any of these strategies to cope, I want you to hear me clearly: there is no judgment here. I know what it feels like to be overwhelmed by anxiety, to crave just a moment of peace, and to reach for whatever is within arm's reach to get it. But these ways of coping are like shadows—they only mask the pain for a while before it seeps back in, often stronger than before.

Please know that there is support for you. These not-so-safe ways aren't solutions; they're signals that something inside you needs attention and care. One of the hardest yet most powerful steps is simply acknowledging them.

You don't have to cope alone. As you read through these sections, be gentle with yourself, take your time, and remember that you are worthy of finding safer, more supportive ways to let out what you're carrying.

Self-Medicating

When anxiety's weight becomes unbearable, it's only natural to want to dull it, even if just for a moment. I know the temptation of reaching for medication or something stronger when that heaviness feels relentless. Self-medicating often starts innocently—an extra glass of wine at dinner to take the edge off, taking a little more than prescribed, or mixing over-the-counter meds in hopes of creating a stronger effect.

In these moments, it can feel like you're finding a brief peace in the storm.

However, as the Swiss physician Paracelsus once said, "The difference between a medicine and a poison is in the dosage." And when we're desperate for relief, it's easy to cross that line. What begins as a quick fix can soon become dependency—reaching for pills, alcohol, or other substances to numb overwhelming emotions. The body adapts quickly, and what once brought relief may no longer work as well. The urge to take "just a little more" can become stronger, leading down a path that often deepens anxiety, adds new health issues and complicates the very emotions we're trying to manage.

Self-medicating is complex because it often feels like it works in the moment. It dulls the pain, blurs the sharp edges of anxiety, and brings that sought-after calm. But self-medicating doesn't address the root of the pain—it only covers it up. And, like a festering wound hidden beneath a bandage, unaddressed pain has a way of growing and resurfacing with greater intensity over time.

If you're reading this and feel a stirring within you about your own habits—a nightly drink that's become several, prescription meds you rely on to get through the day, or even recreational drugs to escape— please know there's no shame here. Self-medicating is a deeply human response to overwhelming pain. Many reach for whatever feels like a lifeline when anxiety takes hold. But I gently want to remind you that this path, while offering short-term relief, can lead to deeper layers of struggle, both physically and emotionally. And deep down, you know this, don't you?

If your current medication isn't working or you find yourself needing more than prescribed, let this be a sign to reach out—not to judge yourself, but to seek support. Speak to a healthcare professional.

Advocate for yourself and your mental health. And if you don't feel heard, find someone who will listen. There is strength in asking for help and choosing a path that allows for safe, supported healing.

Remember, there are safer and more sustainable ways to find relief—paths that don't numb your feelings but help you work through them, transforming anxiety into something you can understand and manage rather than something you need to escape.

Alcohol

Let me share something personal: my relationship with alcohol was one of the most hidden parts of my anxiety. I didn't even realise it had become a coping mechanism until much later when the pattern was firmly in place. From the outside, it looked like unwinding after a long day. In reality? I was using alcohol to numb my thoughts, to fill the silence in my mind, when I finally stopped focusing on everyone and everything else.

Here's what my days used to look like: I would come home after a 10–12-hour workday, attend to my family, handle household chores, and put everyone's needs ahead of my own. I was a high-functioning, anxious person—always busy, always on the go. And then, at the end of the night, I would sit at my laptop and work late, catching up on the responsibilities of my senior role. As long as I kept my mind busy, there was no space for my thoughts to spiral.

But eventually, the day would wind down. The house would go quiet. I'd close my laptop, and that's when the silence would hit—anxiety flooding my mind, filling all the empty spaces. And in those moments, I didn't want to hear my thoughts or sit with the discomfort swirling around in my head. So, I reached for alcohol.

Two or three drinks every night might not sound like much, but it was the way I was drinking them. I would down all three drinks within about 20 minutes, wanting the effect to hit hard and fast, needing to drown out my thoughts just to find a way to sleep. It wasn't about enjoying a drink; it was about turning off the noise in my head. And for a while, it seemed to work. But the cost was high. It wasn't good for my body, and it certainly wasn't good for my mind. The alcohol disrupted my sleep—the very thing I craved most—and masked the deeper issues I needed to face.

It's been around three years since I last had an alcoholic drink. Not because I think alcohol is inherently bad; I believe everything has a place in moderation. But I needed to change my relationship with it. I realised that if I wanted to heal, I needed to find a different way to cope. My journey away from alcohol was about reclaiming the part of me that deserved genuine peace, not temporary numbing.

If alcohol has become part of your story, I want you to know that change is possible. The first step is to become conscious of the relationship you have with it.

Ask yourself: *What does alcohol give me? What do I want my relationship with it to be?* Awareness is the first step to change, but you already know that, don't you?

Illicit Drugs

Maybe you're reading this and thinking, "I don't have an addiction," or maybe you view your drug use as "purely recreational." If that's how you feel, I honour your perspective—there's no judgment here. I respect where you are, and I know you're doing your best to navigate life. But if you're here, reading these words, there might be a part of you wondering why you're reaching for substances more often than you'd like to admit, why the anxiety feels so heavy that sometimes the only relief is to find something—anything—that numbs the pain.

I understand that sometimes life can feel unbearable. Anxiety can be overwhelming, the thoughts never-ending. There are times when the silence feels too loud, and the idea of sitting alone with your thoughts seems impossible. Drugs can feel like a lifeline—a way to escape, to dull the edges of anxiety. Maybe it started occasionally, just to relax and take the edge off. But slowly, without even realising it, the need for that escape grew. A few moments of relief turned into a pattern until it felt like the only way to feel okay was to reach for that substance.

Client Story - *Finding Freedom Beyond Addiction*

I once worked with a client who found herself in this very place. For years, she struggled with an addiction to methamphetamines. She desperately wanted to break free but felt trapped, unable to imagine life without it. She had tried therapy, checked into rehab centres, and stayed clean for weeks at a time—but the urge to use gnawed at her, especially in the quiet moments alone.

Her world was falling apart around her. Family and friends kept their distance, unsure if they could trust her. Even her children found refuge with other family members. She felt isolated, ashamed, and overwhelmed. The more disconnected she felt, the stronger the pull toward the drug became. It was her way of escaping the unbearable anxiety and trying to find calm when nothing else seemed to work.

When we began working together, it wasn't about the drugs. It rarely is about the drugs. It was about her pain—the pain she was trying to soothe and when she felt the strongest need to use. We traced her story back to her childhood, to a time when life felt out of control. Her parents' divorce and remarriages brought new siblings, stepfamilies, and an unspoken expectation for her to be "okay." She became highly attuned to her parents' needs, supporting them in their struggles, but felt she had no one to turn to for her own comfort. Lost and confused, she coped by escaping into books and imaginary worlds and, later, into more numbing behaviours like overeating, TV, alcohol, and eventually, drugs.

Together, we explored that little girl's world—the confusion, the loneliness, the need to belong. We unearthed the beliefs she formed about herself: that she had to be the strong one, holding it together for everyone else, while feeling she didn't belong anywhere. As we untangled those beliefs, her need to numb the pain began to soften. Gradually, she found a way to give that young girl what she had always needed—love, understanding, and permission to feel pain without needing to escape from it.

The last I heard, my client had been drug-free for more than three years. She'd found fulfilling work, rebuilt her relationship with her children, and was living with a new partner who supported her journey. But more than that, she had begun to reclaim herself, finding peace without needing to numb her feelings.

Self-harm of Any Kind

Including this section wasn't easy. Self-harm is complex and deeply personal, and it's not something I've experienced in the most common sense. While I've neglected my own well-being in moments of extreme anxiety, I haven't turned to physical pain to cope. But this book isn't about me—it's about you. And I know that, for many, self-harm is a very real, hidden struggle. So, it felt important to talk about this openly and without judgment, acknowledging what often goes unspoken.

If you're here, it might be because self-harm is part of your life, or perhaps you're trying to understand why someone would choose to hurt themselves. Either way, this is a safe space—a place to explore the roots of self-harm and its connection to anxiety and pain. And if self-harm is your struggle, please know that you're not broken, and there is hope for finding a path that doesn't involve hurting yourself.

Self-harm can take many forms—not just cutting or burning, but also hitting walls, picking at skin, pulling hair, or even denying oneself food. For some, it might show up as reckless behaviour, like excessive drinking, drug use, or impulsive actions that bring feelings of shame. Self-harm often feels like a release, a way to turn emotional pain into something visible, but it's ultimately a "not-so-safe" coping strategy. The relief it brings is only temporary, and the pain often returns with more intensity, reinforcing a painful cycle.

The reasons behind self-harm are varied. It can be tied to trauma, low self-esteem, mental health struggles, or challenging relationships. Sometimes, it's an attempt to punish oneself or express emotions that feel impossible to put into words. But remember, self-harm is a behaviour— it's not who you are. And in the language of NLP, behaviours reveal what a person needs. Every behaviour, even self-harm, has a positive intention behind it—a way to release something that needs to be expressed. But it's not the only way, and it's not a safe way.

Violent or Destructive Behaviour

If you've ever found yourself lashing out—slamming doors, shouting words that sting, or breaking something in a fit of rage—you're probably familiar with the shame that follows. That sinking feeling when the dust settles and the adrenaline fades, leaving only emptiness and regret. It may feel like you've lost control, as if you're powerless against it. But here's the secret: you're not. You *can* take control.

Anger is powerful, but it doesn't have to control you. Often, it rises to protect us when we feel threatened, dismissed, or unseen. Anger is usually driven by fear—fear of disrespect, of violated boundaries, of not being valued. It's a force that demands attention, trying to ensure your needs are met. But while anger mobilises us, turning it into violence or destruction isn't a healthy or effective way to communicate. You already know this, don't you?

While it may seem that being louder or more forceful helps you get your needs met, it actually leaves pain unresolved and harms you and those around you. This pattern often repeats because it addresses only the surface frustration, not the root cause.

So, let's get curious about anger. Instead of focusing on what went wrong, ask yourself: *What did I need in that moment? What was my anger trying to achieve?* Sit with a recent outburst and explore the feelings beneath the rage. Was it fear? A feeling of powerlessness? Frustration at not being heard? Try to wind your mind back to the *moment before* the anger erupted. What were you telling yourself? Remember, even destructive behaviours have a positive intention. Anger is trying to tell you something. It may be pointing to a deeper need that's calling for acknowledgment.

The way you release anger today shapes your tomorrow. Healthy physical outlets like throwing rocks into a lake, hitting a pillow, or screaming into the wind can provide release without harm. But when anger leads to slamming doors, breaking things, or using hurtful words or actions, it leaves lasting impacts on your future, on relationships, and on your own self-image.

I understand the struggle. I've been there—stomping, shouting, and feeling the emptiness afterwards. Those outbursts didn't reflect who I truly was; they reflected a fearful part of me that didn't know another way to cope. If this resonates with you, please know that you have the power to change. Every pause in the heat of the moment is a chance to choose differently.

Start today. If you've made mistakes with your anger, let today be the day you break the cycle. The next time anger rises, take a single, conscious breath. That breath may not erase your anger, but it creates a space to choose—an opportunity to respond differently, to honour your needs without harming yourself or others. Every moment of anger will pass, even if it feels unbearable in the moment.

You are in control of your mind and, therefore, your actions. The future you create starts with the relationship you choose to have with anger. Let's make that relationship one of curiosity and self-compassion. Let's work together to understand what your anger is trying to communicate, then find healthier ways to meet that need.

Does This Sound Anything Like What You are Experiencing?

If you're reading this and any of it resonates, know that I'm here. It's okay if you don't have all the answers. The path forward isn't always clear, but it starts with acknowledging the pain beneath the surface that deserves your attention. Drugs may feel like a lifeline, but true healing comes from understanding and addressing the deeper wound you're trying to soothe.

You are stronger than you know. And no matter where you are right now, it is possible to find peace—one step, one breath, one moment of self-compassion at a time.

Exploring the Need Behind These Behaviours

What is the need behind these behaviours? What is your pain trying to tell you? Whether it's self-harm, alcohol, self-medicating, or another coping mechanism, each action is often trying to serve a purpose—even if it feels destructive. If you recognise yourself in any of these descriptions, I invite you to pause and get curious about what these behaviours might be communicating. When does the urge to reach for these coping mechanisms speak the loudest? Is it when you feel alone? When anxiety overwhelms you? When expressing your needs feels impossible?

Often, this voice is younger than we realise—like a scared child or a frustrated teenager who doesn't know how to be heard. Each behaviour is an attempt to meet a need or express an emotion that feels inexpressible. Rather than acting on the urge, try listening to it. What words, feelings, or memories surface when you sit with it?

Let's start small. Instead of reaching for that familiar coping strategy, try writing down whatever surfaces—your thoughts, emotions, even the messy parts that feel too big to hold. You might find that the urge to self-soothe, however intense, is simply asking to be understood. By recognising these needs, you open up a space for healing and for finding new, supportive ways to cope.

Reflection Questions:

1. *When I feel the urge to reach for this behaviour, what am I truly feeling or needing?*

2. *What alternatives could help me address this need in a way that supports my well-being?*

This process isn't about perfect answers; it's about learning to listen with compassion, giving yourself the chance to explore healthier ways to meet your needs, one small step at a time.

Finding a Different Path to Relief

The path to healing isn't about silencing or shaming that voice—it's about listening and responding with care. Over time, we can explore together what that voice needs to feel understood, safe, and relieved without self-harm. I am right here with you, and I know there are ways to release your pain that don't leave you feeling empty or ashamed.

You deserve to find peace, learn how to hold your emotions with compassion, and let them go in ways that honour your worth. There is a path to healing that will allow you to release what's inside, side by side with support, without causing harm to yourself. And we will walk that path together.

Releasing Moves Us Forward

In therapy, the journey to healing starts with fully unpacking what's happening within us—the behaviours, thoughts, and emotions we carry, both consciously and unconsciously. By exploring the ways anxiety shows up in your life and how you've tried to let it out—whether safely or not—you're bringing awareness to what's really going on inside. And that's why it's so important to get it all out, to name and acknowledge every aspect of your struggle because you can't heal what you don't see.

And the good news? You've already been unknowingly working through the first stage of the model I'm about to introduce to you—CALM. It's a framework I designed to help navigate any challenging situation, but especially to support you in unfolding the wisdom within your anxiety. The first step of this model is Consciousness: becoming aware of your anxiety, its impact on your life, and the ways you've been managing it. By consciously examining all of this, you're taking the first crucial steps toward untangling its hold on you.

The journey we've just taken together through these last chapters has likely stirred up a lot within you—memories, realisations, and maybe even some hope. So take a moment to pause, breathe, and check in with yourself. Perhaps now is a good time to grab a cup of whatever brings you joy, to reflect on what you've uncovered, or simply to let it all settle. Or, if you're feeling energised to learn more and eager to uncover deeper insights, read on.

Either way, you're ready to move forward—to explore the deeper roots of your anxiety, to learn from what it's asking of you, and to begin the journey toward allowing, learning, and ultimately moving toward a more peaceful and empowered life. The CALM model is here to guide you, step by step, as we continue to unfold the wisdom hidden in your anxiety.

As we pause here, you might notice a gentle lightness within you... a sense of 'calm' already in the early stages of unfoldment... like the soft exhale of a deep breath you've been holding for months, maybe years, quietly reminding you that a new way of being is not only possible—it's already beginning to take shape.

CHAPTER 4

The CALM Model: A Pathway Back to Yourself

"We delight in the beauty of the butterfly, but rarely admit the changes it has gone through to achieve that beauty."

~ Maya Angelou

Anxiety can feel overwhelming. In those intense moments, it's challenging to think clearly or make sense of what's happening in your mind and body. I know this feeling all too well—both from my own experiences and from the countless clients who have shared their struggles, searching for stability in the midst of their anxiety.

That's why I developed the CALM model. I wanted to create something that could be easily remembered when anxiety pulls you off course—a simple, powerful word that acts like a beacon, guiding you back to yourself. CALM is more than just a comforting phrase; it's a structured pathway designed to help you regain control, reconnect with your breath and body, and find a place of clarity.

When anxiety takes hold, thoughts often spiral before we even realise it. We can become trapped in a sea of "what ifs" and worst-case scenarios, which only intensifies the anxiety. Many of my clients have shared how helpless they feel in these moments, as though their minds are racing beyond control. This is where the CALM model steps in. CALM provides a structured, grounded pathway through anxious moments, helping you reconnect with yourself and your surroundings. Whether you're facing a specific anxious moment or experiencing an ongoing state of anxiety, the CALM model offers a way to find balance.

I created CALM to offer something tangible that clients could hold onto in their most difficult moments—when it's hard even to remember how to breathe, let alone think clearly. CALM is a tool for breaking the cycle of anxious thoughts, helping you feel grounded and regain a sense of control. In my own journey with anxiety, I've learned that awareness is the foundation of transformation. This is why CALM begins with Consciousness—the essential first step in reclaiming your mind from anxiety.

The CALM model grew out of the foundation I built through my training with Dr. Heidi Heron at the NLP Worldwide Institutes of Training. There, I learned how to guide clients from their current state to their desired state by removing obstacles and building resources. While the insights I gained were transformative, I wanted to adapt what I'd learned into something that could be easily remembered and applied in the moment. CALM, as a word, carries both a sense of peace and a reminder to take meaningful steps forward.

Each step of CALM—Consciousness, Allow, Learn, and Move—is designed to help you transform anxious moments so you can meet anxiety with curiosity and empowerment. In the sections that follow, we'll explore each step, building a toolkit you can turn to whenever you need to reconnect with your inner calm.

What is CALM?

CALM is both an acronym and a roadmap—a simple structure to guide you back to yourself when anxiety starts to take over. Let's break down what each step stands for:

- **Consciousness:** The first step is becoming aware of your thoughts and emotions. When you feel anxiety rising, ask yourself: *What am I noticing right now? What thoughts are racing through my mind?* This awareness—this consciousness—helps you observe your experience without judgment, creating distance from the swirl of anxious thoughts.

- **Allow:** Once you're aware of what's happening, the next step is to allow yourself to feel it. Instead of resisting the anxiety, give yourself permission to acknowledge what's there. Often, we try to avoid our anxiety by staying busy, but in allowing it, we let ourselves simply be with the feeling. This may feel uncomfortable at first, but allowing your emotions to exist without judgment is crucial to understanding their role in your experience. Ask yourself, *Where am I noticing my discomfort? What is it like to just stay with and allow this feeling? What am I noticing about my resistance to feeling this discomfort?*

- **Learn:** This is where we start to gain insights from our anxiety. Every emotion, including anxiety, has something to teach us. It may point to an unmet need, an old wound, or a belief that's ready for exploration. In this step, you might ask yourself: *When did I first start feeling this way? What might I need right now? What is feeling this way allowing me?* Sometimes, anxiety is trying to protect you in ways that no longer serve you. Learning allows you to recognise these patterns and begin transforming your relationship with anxiety.

- **Move:** The final step is moving forward with empowered actions. Now that you're aware, you've allowed the emotions, and you've learned from them, it's time to take small, intentional steps toward the state you want to be in. Ask yourself, *What steps can I take to move toward my desired state? What resources do I need?* Moving forward might mean reaching out for support, practising grounding techniques, or making decisions aligned with the life you want to live.

Each letter in CALM represents a key step in regaining clarity and control. Whether you're in the middle of a moment of anxiety or reflecting on it afterwards, the CALM model gives you a flexible, accessible tool to use anytime you need to reconnect with a sense of calm.

A Quick, Grounding Mantra

The CALM model isn't just a tool—it's a mantra you can turn to anytime anxiety arises. When you start to feel anxious, remember the word CALM as a simple, guiding prompt:

- **C** — *Consciousness:* Notice what you're feeling right now. Name the thoughts and emotions present in this moment.

- **A** — *Allow:* Give yourself permission to feel the anxiety without judgment. Let it be there for now without needing to change it.

- **L** — *Learn:* Ask yourself what this feeling might be telling you. Is there an underlying need or message?

- **M** — *Move:* Take a small step forward. This might mean grounding yourself, reaching out, or simply breathing deeply.

Think of CALM as a pathway that guides you back to yourself, one step at a time. Each letter can help you find clarity and regain a sense of control, whether in a specific moment or over days, as you work through deeper layers of anxiety. It's a flexible tool designed to meet you wherever you are.

Your First Assignment: Begin Practicing CALM

Now that you've been introduced to the CALM model, it's time to put it into practice. Begin using CALM as a grounding mantra whenever you feel anxiety rising. Start with the first step—consciousness—and simply observe your thoughts and feelings without judgment. Notice what arises and let yourself be curious. This is where your journey begins.

Consciousness: Observing Your Experience

Description and Purpose

Consciousness is the first step of CALM. When anxiety arises, this step focuses on bringing awareness to your inner experience—what thoughts, sensations, and emotions are present. Observing without judgment allows you to take a step back, creating some distance from the intensity of the anxiety.

Thought Starters

- What thoughts immediately come to mind when anxiety begins?

- What physical sensations do you notice? Where in your body do you feel them?

Activity: Becoming Conscious of Your Anxiety

1. **Find a Quiet Place**

   Choose a space where you can be alone and undisturbed for a few minutes.

2. **Recall a Moment of Anxiety**

   Close your eyes and recall a recent time when you felt anxious. Picture it as clearly as you can, observing the moment with calm curiosity.

3. **Ask Yourself These Questions**

   - Where in my body does the anxiety show up? My chest, stomach, or throat?

   - How does it move? Quickly, like a wave? Or more slowly and subtly?

- How does it feel at first, and does it change over time?

4. **Simply Observe**

Let yourself become an observer of your experience. There's no right or wrong way to feel. You're just becoming aware of what anxiety feels like for you.

5. **Journal Your Observations**

After a few minutes, write down your observations in a journal. This initial awareness is the foundation for managing anxiety with greater clarity.

Remember: There's no need to change anything right now. Simply observe. Consciousness is the first step in understanding and responding to your anxiety with awareness.

Allow: Making Space for Your Anxiety

Description and Purpose

Once you're aware of your anxiety, the next step is to allow it to be there without trying to resist or push it away. Allowing means giving yourself permission to feel the discomfort instead of avoiding it. This can feel counterintuitive, but letting anxiety be present without judgment can reduce its intensity over time.

Thought Starters

- How do I usually respond when I feel anxious?

- What happens when I allow myself to simply feel the anxiety without resistance?

Activity: Being with Your Anxiety

1. **Find a Quiet Space**

   As before, choose a place where you won't be disturbed.

2. **Recall an Anxious Moment**

   Take a few deep breaths, close your eyes, and recall a specific anxious moment. Imagine this moment calmly, observing what feelings arise.

3. **Notice How Anxiety Feels**

   Pay attention to where the anxiety arises in your body. Does it start in one spot, or does it spread? Allow these sensations to exist without judgment.

4. **Stay with the Discomfort**

   For a few moments, stay with the feeling. Notice if you want to distract yourself, but instead, keep observing. Ask yourself: What happens if I simply stay with this feeling?

5. **Journal Your Observations**

   When you're ready, open your eyes and take a few moments to journal what came up. How did it feel to simply be with your anxiety without pushing it away?

Why Allowing Matters:

Allowing your anxiety to exist without trying to fix or escape it can be empowering. This practice teaches your mind and body that you can handle the discomfort, making anxiety feel less overwhelming over time.

Learn: Becoming Curious About Your Anxiety

Description and Purpose

Now that you've observed and allowed your anxiety, the next step is to learn from it. This involves shifting from passive observation to active curiosity—asking what your anxiety might be trying to communicate. Every emotion, including anxiety, often signals deeper needs, fears, or beliefs.

Thought Starters

- What might this anxiety be telling me about my needs?

- Are there specific situations that trigger my anxiety more than others?

Activity: Learning from Your Anxiety

1. **Recall the Anxiety from the Previous Exercise**

   Think back to the moment of anxiety you allowed yourself to feel earlier.

2. **Shift into Curiosity**

   Ask yourself: What is this anxiety trying to tell me? Is there something it wants me to pay attention to?

3. **Consider its Origins**

   Reflect on when this kind of anxiety first appeared in your life. Was it in response to a particular experience or situation? Understanding these roots can provide valuable insights.

4. Ask Questions to Your Anxiety

Try asking:

- What purpose did you serve when you first appeared?

- What do you believe your role is in my life today?

- Is there something I need to change or address?

5. Journal Your Discoveries

Write down any insights that emerge from this exercise. Reflect on how this knowledge might help you respond differently to anxiety in the future.

Why Learning Matters:

Learning from your anxiety helps you move from fear to understanding. By asking questions, you create a relationship with your anxiety that's based on insight rather than avoidance.

Move: Taking Empowered Action

Description and Purpose

The final step is to move forward with empowered action. This isn't about "fixing" anxiety, but rather making intentional choices that align with the life you want. Moving forward could mean anything from small daily habits to bigger steps toward peace and clarity.

Thought Starters

- What would I like to feel instead of anxiety?

- What small actions can I take to move toward this feeling?

Exercise: Moving Forward with Empowered Actions

1. **Reflect on What You've Learned**

   Consider the insights you gained in the Learn exercise. What did you discover about the purpose of your anxiety? Ground yourself in this awareness before moving forward.

2. **Identify Your Desired State**

   If you're experiencing anxiety, what would you prefer to feel instead? Calm, confidence, peace? Write down this desired state to clarify your intention.

3. **Brainstorm Small Steps Toward This State**

   Think of small, manageable actions that align with this feeling. For example:

   - Practicing breathing exercises
   - Taking short walks to centre yourself
   - Scheduling moments of relaxation
   - Speaking kindly to yourself when self-doubt arises

4. **Consider Support Resources**

   What resources might help you? Whether it's a mindfulness app, supportive friends, or professional guidance, list any supports that could help you reach your goals.

5. **Commit to One Action Today**

   Choose one small action you can take today. Acknowledge yourself for this step, no matter how minor it may feel—every action builds momentum.

6. Journal Your Action Plan

Write down your desired state, steps, and resources. This serves as a reminder of your path forward.

Why Movement Matters:

Taking small, intentional actions builds new pathways toward peace, clarity, and balance. As you practice, anxiety will loosen its grip, and you'll grow more confident in your ability to navigate it.

Final Thoughts on CALM

The CALM model is more than just a sequence of steps; it's a practice that helps you reconnect with yourself, especially in moments when anxiety feels overwhelming. Each step—Consciousness, Allow, Learn, and Move—guides you through a process of self-awareness and acceptance, transforming how you experience and respond to anxiety. By taking these steps, you're building a pathway back to calm, one that you can rely on whenever you need it.

Remember, learning to navigate anxiety is a journey. Some days, you might feel empowered and grounded, while other days, you may still feel challenged. That's okay. Each time you practice CALM, you strengthen your ability to respond to anxiety with intention and compassion. Give yourself permission to take it one step at a time.

In the next chapter, we'll explore a new way of seeing anxiety—one that goes beyond fear and discomfort to reveal the insights and growth it can offer. By shifting our perspective, we can start to understand anxiety as a part of our experience that holds valuable information. The CALM model will serve as your foundation as we explore these deeper insights, helping you develop a relationship with anxiety that's rooted in understanding rather than avoidance.

Take a moment to appreciate the steps you've taken in this chapter. You're on a path of self-discovery, learning to view and manage anxiety in a way that's compassionate, intentional, and empowering.

CHAPTER 5

Viewing Anxiety from a Different Perspective

"The map is not the territory. People respond to their perception of reality, not reality itself."

~ NLP Presupposition

When you're in the midst of anxiety, it often feels like there's only one way to look at the situation—your way. In those moments, your perspective narrows, making everything feel immediate, urgent, and overwhelming. Have you ever noticed how hard it is to think clearly when you're anxious? That's because anxiety limits our ability to step back and see things from different viewpoints. And when our view is restricted, so are our choices.

Why does perspective matter so much when navigating anxiety? People respond to their own perceptions of reality, and when we're wrapped up in anxious thoughts, that reality can become distorted. The choices we think we have may feel small or sometimes like there's no choice at all. But what if there's more to the situation than meets the eye?

One of the main principles of NLP (Neuro-Linguistic Programming) is expanding choice. By shifting perspective, NLP helps us see the whole picture rather than just a small, stress-filled fragment of it. This is one reason I love using it in my practice—it allows people to shift how they see their challenges, bringing in new insights and opening up more freedom in how they respond.

When anxiety hits, it can be challenging to remember that we can look at things from another angle. Anxiety draws us so deeply into our experience that we often forget how much more information is available if we just zoom out. What would happen if you could see yourself from a distance in those anxious moments? What if you become the observer of your own experience? Sometimes, simply viewing yourself from a detached perspective can change how you approach the entire situation.

As we move forward, let's explore how shifting perspective can help you navigate anxiety. You might discover that looking at your experience from a different angle opens up new choices and helps you see the bigger picture.

Client Story - *Shifting Perspectives to Find Connection*

I once worked with a client who came to me seeking help with her addiction. Alongside her struggles, she had a long-standing tension with her younger brother, whom she felt judged by and distant from. She believed she was the "black sheep" of the family and couldn't understand why her brother remained emotionally unavailable, even though she deeply desired a close relationship with him. She thought *We're family, after all—how can he be so cold?*

In our sessions, I encouraged her to step back from the situation and look at it as if she were a complete stranger—someone who didn't know anyone involved. I guided her to view her brother, herself, and even her parents from this objective, detached perspective. This practice is what we call *perceptual positions* in NLP.

As she began to step into her brother's perspective, a whole new picture emerged. For the first time, she considered what it must have been like for him. She realised that her brother had endured years of "losing" her to addiction. From his perspective, it was as though he had been protecting himself from the pain of getting close, only to be hurt again if her addiction returned. She understood that his distance wasn't about judgment or rejection—it was a way of shielding himself from further heartache.

How would it feel to see a relationship from a new angle like this? For my client, this shift in perspective changed everything. She could finally see her brother's behaviour as an attempt at self-protection, not an expression of indifference. With this new understanding, she was able to approach him with more compassion, breaking down the barriers that had kept them apart for so long.

Sometimes, taking a step back and viewing things from another's perspective can open up a new world of understanding. What relationships in your own life might benefit from a fresh viewpoint? This exercise may reveal that the distance or tension isn't as personal as it feels—it may simply be someone's way of managing their own pain.

Reflective Exercises: Shifting Your Perspective

In this exercise, we'll practice stepping out of our current perspective to view ourselves and our anxiety from different angles. This shift can help us gain fresh insights into our experience.

1. **Identify Your Current Situation**

   Start by thinking about something specific you're feeling anxious or confused about. It could be an event, a recurring situation, or even anxiety itself. Let yourself become conscious of this experience. *What thoughts or feelings arise as you focus on it?*

2. **Zoom Out from Your Experience**

   Now, imagine zooming out as if you're watching a movie of yourself in this situation. Picture yourself as if you're observing from afar.

   - *What do you notice about your body language and movements?*

   - *How do you appear in this moment—tense, calm, or somewhere in between?*

   Next, notice anyone else who appears in your "movie." Observe how they interact with you or how you respond to them.

- *What do you see in their body language or expressions?*

- *Is there anything they say or don't say that stands out?*

Observe this scene as neutrally as possible, letting go of judgments. *What does this distant perspective reveal to you about your reactions or interactions?*

3. **Move to a New Perspective**

   Imagine yourself sitting in a different seat in the movie theatre. This time, you're a complete stranger watching someone you don't know on the screen—someone simply navigating their day. You don't have any backstory or specific insight; you're just observing this person (yourself) in the present moment.

   - *How does this person appear to you? Do they seem nervous, confident, or uncertain? What observations lead you to this conclusion?*

   - If you feel comfortable, try shifting to the perspective of others in the scene. *What might they be feeling or noticing as they interact with you in this situation?*

4. **Offer Advice as a Stranger**

   Returning to the stranger's perspective, imagine offering the person on the screen some advice.

   - *If you could say one thing to them, what would it be?*

   - *What do you think they (you) might need to hear right now?*

   - Is there anything you can notice from this distant perspective that they (you) might not be able to see up close?

This advice could be practical, compassionate, or simply reassuring. Write down any insights that come to you as you step outside your own perspective.

5. Return to Yourself

Finally, bring your focus back to yourself and reflect on what you've observed.

- *What have you learned from this exercise?*

- *Has seeing yourself from a distance shifted anything for you?*

- *Are there any new choices or actions you could take to approach this situation differently?*

Take a moment to journal your observations. Write down any new perspectives, insights, or shifts in feeling that emerged as you stepped out of your usual viewpoint. How do you feel about the situation now that you've seen it from multiple angles?

Why Perspective Matters

When we're deep in anxiety, it can feel like we have no options and no way out. But by shifting our perspective, we open ourselves up to new possibilities, insights, and ways of responding to life's challenges. The more perspectives we take in, the more choices we have, and with more choices comes more freedom. Remember, anxiety narrows our view—stepping into other perspectives expands it.

Bringing It All Together

As we've explored, shifting perspective can be a powerful tool in managing anxiety. By stepping outside of our immediate experience and viewing situations from different angles, we open ourselves up to new insights, compassion, and a wider range of choices. Just like my client, who saw her relationship with her brother in a new light, we can learn that sometimes the obstacles we face aren't as rigid as they seem.

When anxiety feels like it's closing in, remember that there is often more than one way to view any situation. Taking a step back, observing from a different seat, or even imagining yourself as an outsider can reveal options you might not have considered before. This practice not only helps in managing anxiety but also strengthens your resilience and flexibility in the face of life's challenges.

In the next chapter, we'll dive even deeper into ways to view anxiety from new angles, helping you reshape your relationship with it and discover tools to move through it with greater ease. For now, consider how you can apply this shift in perspective to situations in your own life. A new viewpoint may reveal that you have more choices—and more freedom—than you realised.

CHAPTER 6

Engaging with Anxiety: Understanding Distance, Beliefs, and Behaviours

"Until you make the unconscious conscious, it will direct your life, and you will call it Fate."

~ Carl Jung

When we talk about being *associated* with something, it means we are fully immersed in the experience. In the CALM model, this is the *Allowing* stage. When you're associated with an experience, you're seeing, feeling, and hearing everything as if you're right in the middle of it. This can be helpful when you need to be fully engaged—like when I'm writing this book on anxiety or when you're deeply focused on a task. Your world narrows, and you may lose track of time. While everyone's experience is different, this intense focus can be productive in some situations.

But there are also times when being associated can be harmful—especially when we're caught up in anxious thoughts or catastrophising outcomes. When you're fully immersed in those thoughts, they start to feel as if they're real. Your body responds to the emotions as if the worst-case scenario has already happened. Feelings of shame, fear, and dread flood in, making it hard to think clearly. In those moments, being associated with anxiety can actually amplify it.

Here's the empowering part: you have the choice to step back. You can learn to dissociate from these anxious thoughts and observe them from a distance, gaining clarity and perspective. Let's explore what it means to *dissociate* and how it can be a useful tool in managing anxiety.

Electing to Dissociate

So, how do you consciously choose to dissociate from anxious thoughts? And how do you know when it's time to step back?

Your body can act as your guide. When you're fully associated with anxiety, your body may feel like an alarm system, signaling that something is wrong. Perhaps your heart races, your palms get sweaty, or your stomach churns. These are your body's messages, telling you that you're deeply immersed in anxious thoughts.

In those moments, you can choose to step back, observe your thoughts from a distance, and create space between yourself and the anxiety. But before diving into how to dissociate, let's first explore the value of fully associating with your anxiety. Understanding how it feels in your body can help you become more aware of its effects and start to develop curiosity about it.

Reflective Exercises

Visualising "It" (Sense it, locate it, exit it, examine it)

To better understand your anxiety and how it "shows up" for you, let's start by fully associating with it. In this exercise, you'll observe, sense, and tangibly visualise your anxiety.

1. **Go Back to the Feeling**

   Think about a recent moment of anxiety. Recall how it feels and where it seems to "live" in your body. *Is it in your chest, your stomach, or your throat?* Allow yourself to really associate with it now—notice where it feels most intense. Pinpoint its exact location.

2. **Sense the Anxiety**

   Now, imagine you could reach inside and touch your anxiety. *What would it feel like? Does it have a texture? How does it respond to you touching it?* Notice if it's smooth or rough, warm or cold, light or heavy. This step lets you develop a more intimate awareness of the sensations that accompany anxiety.

   • *What do these qualities about your anxiety mean to you?*

3. Visualise It Outside Your Body

Imagine bringing this anxiety out of your body. Visualise it sitting in the palm of your hand. *What does it look like? Does it move, or is it still?* What colour is it? Take some time to truly visualise it and observe all of its details.

Reflection: How does externalising your anxiety make you feel? What do you notice about its appearance?

4. Reflect on the Experience

Now that you can see your anxiety from a bit of distance, take a moment to reflect on it. Ask yourself:

- ***How does this anxiety challenge me?***

- ***What do I believe about it?***

- ***Who would I be without it?***

- ***What do you notice about the space where your anxiety came from now?***

Write down your answers in your journal. This reflection helps you become curious about anxiety and explore its role in your life. By associating with your anxiety and visualising it, you're creating the space to understand it in a new, more insightful way.

Moving from Association to Dissociation

Now that we've practised fully associating with anxiety, let's explore the next powerful step: *dissociation.*

Anxiety often feels overwhelming because we are so close to it—it's as if it's consuming us. Dissociating gives you the ability to step back and observe your thoughts and feelings from a distance. This doesn't mean ignoring or running from them; rather, it's about gaining perspective and reducing the emotional intensity.

Think of the last time you were completely absorbed in anxious thoughts. Maybe it was when someone didn't reply to your text right away, or your boss asked for a meeting without explaining why. Recall how your body reacted: the quickening heart rate, sweaty palms, racing mind. These signals are your body's way of responding to the "threat" your mind has created based on the story you're telling yourself.

Dissociating allows you to step back and see that story for what it is—just a story, not an undeniable truth.

Reflective Exercise: Practicing Dissociation

Let's walk you through an exercise to practice stepping back from your anxiety and observing it from a distance. This process can help you see your emotions with greater clarity and lessen their intensity.

1. **Zoom Out and Observe Yourself**

   Imagine yourself zooming out from this moment of anxiety. Picture it as if you're watching a scene in a movie. Observe how you're reacting—your movements, posture, and behaviour.

   - *What do you notice about how anxiety shows up in your body?*

2. **Zoom Out Even Further**

   Now, imagine taking another step back. This time, picture yourself watching this "movie" from a greater distance. With each step back, you may start to feel less absorbed in the emotions.

   - *How does the intensity of your emotions begin to change?*

3. Keep Zooming Out

Continue zooming out until you're watching yourself, watching yourself, watching the movie. With each layer of distance, notice how the anxiety that once felt so consuming gradually begins to soften.

- *What happens as you keep stepping back? Does the anxiety feel lighter?*

4. Notice the Change

As you observe yourself from this doubly-dissociated place, ask yourself:

- *What is different? How do I feel now compared to when I was fully associated with my anxiety?*

- *What new insights or choices do I have from this perspective?*

5. Journal Your Experience

Once you've completed the exercise, take a moment to journal your observations.

- *How did your body react when you were fully associated? How did it change as you zoomed out and dissociated?*

- *What did you learn about your anxiety through this process?*

Why Both Matter: Association and Dissociation

Both association and dissociation are valuable tools in navigating anxiety. When you're associated, you fully engage with your anxiety, which allows you to understand how it shows up in your body and reflect on the role it plays in your life. Being associated helps you identify the physical and emotional responses that arise in anxious moments.

On the other hand, dissociation allows you to step back and observe your anxiety from a distance. By reducing emotional intensity, you gain clarity and perspective on your thoughts. In moments when anxiety feels overwhelming, knowing how to dissociate can give you the space to choose a new response—moving from fear and overwhelm to empowerment and choice.

Reflection: *How do you feel about using both association and dissociation as tools for understanding your anxiety? Which approach resonates more with you, and when might each be most useful?*

Separating Our Beliefs from Our Feelings & Behaviours

In the previous chapter, we explored how being fully immersed in your thoughts and emotions can sometimes feel overwhelming. We practised dissociating—stepping back to create space between yourself and your anxiety to gain perspective. Now, let's shift to something equally powerful: understanding how to separate your beliefs from your feelings and behaviours.

When you're caught in the thick of anxiety, it can be difficult to tell where one ends and the other begins. You might feel like your anxious thoughts, emotions, and reactions are all tangled together. However, beliefs, feelings, and behaviours are actually distinct from one another. Recognising how they interact—and, more importantly, how to separate them—can help you take back control.

Beliefs shape how we experience anxiety. Often, it's the beliefs we hold about ourselves, the world, or others that trigger anxious feelings. Those feelings, in turn, influence how we act. But what if we could slow things down and notice the beliefs driving those feelings? What if we could examine beliefs that no longer serve us and replace them with ones that do?

▌ Client Story - *A Lesson in Beliefs*

One client, a middle-aged man who led a small team in a large organisation, sat across from me in my practice room. On the surface, he seemed composed—articulate, calm, and professional. But he came to me because he was struggling with anger and impatience, especially when his colleagues disagreed with him.

As he shared his story, it became clear that his calm exterior didn't match what he was feeling inside. He told me that, in moments of disagreement, his face would flush red with anger, his heart would race, and his tone would become stern. He'd respond with things like, "Let's take this offline," or "We don't have time to debate this." He felt defensive, almost as if his colleagues' disagreements were personal attacks.

I asked him what he believed about his colleagues when they disagreed with him. After a pause, he said, "I believe they're challenging me because they don't think I know what I'm doing. They don't believe in me."

This belief—*"They don't believe in me"*—was triggering his anger. But when we examined other areas of his life, he recalled a time when his wife disagreed with his plans. Instead of feeling challenged, he felt supported.

Through our work together, he started to see the difference: he believed his wife's disagreement was intended to help him avoid stress or prevent wasted time, while he believed his colleagues were undermining him. His belief about his wife's support led to different feelings and behaviours than his belief about his colleagues. By working on shifting his beliefs about his colleagues, he began to approach questions and challenges from his team with more ease. He was less personally attached to the questions his team raised and even became grateful that he led a team that felt safe enough to express ideas and concerns. He realised he could apply that same perspective shift with his colleagues.

Reflective Questions:

- *Have you ever reacted strongly to someone's words or actions, only to later realise that your beliefs about their intentions influenced your reaction?*

- *What beliefs might be driving your own reactions to disagreements or challenges?*

Beliefs, Feelings, and Behaviours

This story highlights a key point: beliefs are separate from feelings. However, because beliefs often lead to feelings, they can become so intertwined that we don't even realise it. When we start to separate our beliefs from our feelings, we can see how one influences the other—and then choose to focus on beliefs that serve us better.

Think back to your own moments of anxiety. What beliefs tend to come up in those moments?

- *"I need to get out of here."*

- *"I'm going to embarrass myself."*

- *"Something bad is going to happen."*

- *"What will people think of me?"*

- *"What if I mess up?"*

- *"I can't handle this."*

These beliefs create a narrative in your mind, shaping your feelings of anxiety, which then influence how you behave. In the next chapter, we'll dive even deeper into the stories we tell ourselves, but for now, let's practice separating the beliefs and feelings that arise during anxious moments.

Reflective Exercises: Separating Beliefs and Feelings

This exercise will help you gain clarity by separating your beliefs from the feelings they trigger.

1. **Set Up Your Journal**

   - Turn to a new page in your journal. Draw a line down the middle. Label one column *BELIEFS* and the other *FEELINGS.*

2. **Unpacking Your Feelings**

   - Think back to a recent moment when you felt anxious. In the *FEELINGS* column, write down all the emotions you experienced: fear, nervousness, unease, frustration—anything that came up. Don't hold back.

3. **Unpacking Your Beliefs**

   - In the *BELIEFS* column, list what you believed about the situation that led to those feelings. What were you telling yourself? It might be something like, *"I'm not good enough," "They won't understand,"* or *"I'm going to embarrass myself."* Write down as many beliefs as you can remember.

4. Compare the Lists

- Take a moment to compare the two columns. Notice how specific beliefs triggered specific feelings. This is an important realisation because it shows how quickly beliefs can influence how we feel and act. By slowing down, you can start to untangle the two and see the pattern.

The belief comes first—often so quickly you don't even realise it. Then, the feelings follow, and finally, those feelings drive your behaviours.

Why This Matters

This exercise goes beyond reflection; it's about reclaiming your power. When you recognise and recognise that beliefs create feelings, which in turn shape behaviours, you begin to realise you can change your beliefs. You can choose to focus on beliefs that serve you, rather than those that keep you stuck in fear and anxiety.

Of course, slowing things down isn't always easy in the heat of an anxious moment. But with practice, it can become more natural, even in the most challenging situations.

Reflective Questions: *For now, take a moment to reflect on what you discovered in this exercise. What patterns did you notice in your beliefs and feelings? How might choosing different beliefs change your experience of anxiety?*

Final Thoughts on Empowering Choices with Awareness

Navigating anxiety involves understanding both the ways we experience it up close and how we can step back to gain perspective. By learning to shift between association and dissociation, you gain the flexibility to approach anxious thoughts with curiosity, clarity, and balance. These skills empower you to choose how deeply you engage with your anxiety at any given moment, so it doesn't automatically overwhelm you.

Similarly, recognising the differences between beliefs, feelings, and behaviours gives you more control over your reactions. When you can identify the beliefs fueling your anxiety, you're better equipped to challenge and shift them, freeing yourself from automatic responses that may not serve you. Understanding these connections isn't about suppressing your emotions; it's about creating the space to respond intentionally.

Reflective Questions: Take a moment to consider the tools you've explored in this chapter.

- When might you choose to fully associate with an anxious thought to better understand it?

- When would it serve you to dissociate, stepping back for clarity?

- How might the separation of beliefs, feelings, and behaviours change the way you respond to anxiety?

These skills work together to form a foundation for self-awareness and empowerment, allowing you to approach anxiety with more choice and less fear. In the next chapter, we'll expand on these ideas with insights from Neuro-Linguistic Programming (NLP), a powerful approach for reshaping the beliefs that shape our reality. By practising these tools, you're building a path toward understanding and reshaping the stories you tell yourself—stories that have the power to transform your experience with anxiety.

CHAPTER 7

NLP—How Your Mind Works

"Every thought we think is creating our future."

~ Louise L. Hay

Up to this point, we've explored how beliefs influence feelings and behaviours, and how important it is to separate those beliefs from the emotions that often take hold of us during moments of anxiety. Now, I want to introduce you to one of the most powerful tools I've encountered in my therapeutic practice: Neuro-Linguistic Programming, or NLP.

My Introduction to NLP

When I first stumbled upon Neuro-Linguistic Programming (NLP), I had already gained a wealth of insights from tools like Louise Hay's *You Can Heal Your Life* and the Enneagram. Both had helped me explore the roots of my hypervigilance, anxiety, and deep-seated fears of abandonment stemming from childhood. Through these resources, I began to understand my patterns and emotions on a new level. Meditations and affirmations became integral to my daily routine, and for a while, I felt that I was making real progress in my personal growth.

Yet, some deeply rooted behaviours refused to shift—like my lingering avoidance of commitment to social events and my constant worrying about my children. No matter how many affirmations I repeated, these habits remained resiliently in place.

As I neared the end of my role as CEO, the inevitable question of "what's next?" surfaced, triggering familiar waves of anxiety. The uncertainty brought back a sense of foreboding, and I found myself feeling stuck. That's when a colleague brought up NLP again. I had heard of it before, but the cost of training had always seemed out of reach. Now, with a bit of extra time and resources, I decided to revisit it, so I did a quick search online.

The first result was NLP Worldwide Institutes of Training (thankfully!). After a few days of back-and-forth, I had my initial call with Bianca. It was one of the most meaningful conversations I'd ever experienced—Bianca was genuinely interested in me. Her questions were thoughtful, and she listened deeply, leaving me feeling truly seen and understood. By the end of the call, I had booked my first training, and from that moment on, I was hooked.

NLP quickly became a comprehensive toolkit, not only enhancing my work with clients but also helping me navigate my own inner complexities. It showed me how my thoughts, language, and behaviours were intricately linked—and, most importantly, it gave me tools to break free from anxiety's grip. Today, I'm able to help others do the same, empowering them to overcome their own challenges just as I did.

What is NLP?

Neuro-Linguistic Programming, or NLP, stands for:

- **Neuro:** Refers to our nervous system—the network through which our brain processes everything we see, hear, feel, smell, and taste. At the centre of this system, the brain generates thoughts that produce emotions, creating chemicals that impact our body. Imagine your nervous system as an intricate magnetic field charged by the chemicals produced in response to your thoughts and emotions.

- **Linguistic:** Refers to the language we use to describe our experiences, both verbally and non-verbally. Language shapes how we make sense of the world, how we communicate with others, and how we process our internal dialogue. Every word we use, along with our tone and pace of speech, influences how we program our minds.

- **Programming:** Refers to the unconscious strategies or "programs" we develop over time to navigate different situations. We each have programs for handling stress, conflict, decision-making, and much more. Like any program, these can be changed and updated.

NLP emerged in the 1970s and was developed by John Grinder, Richard Bandler, and Frank Pucilek, who studied and modelled the work of influential therapists like Virginia Satir and Milton Erickson. Originally designed as a model for effective communication, thinking, and change, NLP has evolved to include techniques that enable transformation on the deepest levels of the unconscious mind.

The Power of Your Three Minds

A core principle in NLP is understanding the different roles of our three levels of mind: the conscious mind, the unconscious mind, and the higher consciousness. Each plays a unique role in shaping our experiences and responses.

The Conscious Mind

Remember when you first learned to drive or ride a bike? You had to consciously think about every step: "Press the clutch, release it slowly, check the mirrors." This part of your mind analyses, plans, and even provides that internal dialogue—"You're running late" or "Why did you say that?" It helps you complete daily tasks like budgeting or grocery shopping and is called the conscious mind because you're aware of its presence.

The Unconscious Mind

Your unconscious mind is a vast storehouse of memories—everything you've seen, heard, felt, tasted, or smelled is filed away here. Unlike the conscious mind, the unconscious isn't analytical; it operates based on patterns and associations formed over time. Think of it as the home of habits.

The unconscious mind's main role is to keep you safe. It takes everything literally, which is why what you say to yourself matters. If you're constantly thinking, "I'm a failure," or "I can't do this," your unconscious will accept these as truths. This is why speaking to yourself in terms of what you *want* rather than what you *don't want* is so impactful.

The unconscious also protects us by repressing memories that it deems too challenging until we're ready to handle them. This is why trauma survivors may not recall certain events until they've developed enough inner resources to confront those memories.

The Higher Conscious Mind

This is the part of you that connects to something beyond yourself—whether it's a "thank you" whispered after finding a parking spot in a crowded lot or a moment of intuition that steers you away from danger. It's the part that taps into your sense of spirituality or the energy that flows through all things, whether you define it as God, Buddha, the universe, or simply the flow of life.

Higher consciousness is the source of wisdom we access in moments of stillness, such as during meditation, a quiet walk, or even a shower. It reminds us that we're part of something greater and that this source of strength is always available to us.

Why NLP Matters in Healing Anxiety

NLP helps you understand how your mind processes information and how your language and beliefs shape your experiences. By gaining insight into how these "programs" work, you gain the power to change them. Anxiety often comes from deeply rooted patterns of thought and behaviour, but with the right tools, those patterns can be rewritten.

NLP goes beyond learning new coping strategies—it's about understanding the inner workings of your mind so you can take control of it. By shifting your thoughts and beliefs, you can change the way you feel and act, which is where the real power of NLP lies.

Reflective Exercise: Observing Your Unconscious Programs

Let's take a closer look at how your unconscious mind operates. Start by thinking back to a recent moment when you felt anxious and write down the specific thoughts that were racing through your mind. Then, ask yourself:

- *What do I believe about this situation?*

- *Where did this belief come from?*

- *How do I know it's true?*

- *What different perspective might I have not considered?*

Notice how quickly your unconscious mind jumps to conclusions. Now, choose one belief you'd like to change. Instead of focusing on what you *don't* want, reframe the belief in a positive way. For instance, instead of "I don't want to be anxious," try "I want to feel calm and grounded."

This is the beginning of reprogramming your unconscious mind. As we continue through this chapter, we'll explore NLP techniques to help you transform your experience with anxiety on a deeper level.

How NLP Works: The Communication Model and Its Power

In the previous chapter, we examined how beliefs shape our feelings and behaviours. Now, let's explore how our minds actually process experiences. Understanding this is key to understanding why we react the way we do, and this is where Neuro-Linguistic Programming (NLP) comes in.

Before I discovered NLP, I had already immersed myself in self-help, including Louise Hay's *You Can Heal Your Life* and the Enneagram. These tools helped me recognise how childhood abandonment issues contributed to my hypervigilance, and they gave me insights that transformed my life. Yet, even with all this knowledge, certain habits clung on: avoidance, commitment issues, and social anxiety.

NLP felt like the missing key. It didn't just help me understand my thoughts and behaviours; it provided a way to shift them. For the first time, I realised I wasn't at the mercy of my experiences—I had a toolkit to change them. NLP wasn't just another meditation or affirmation; it was a structured, practical framework for lasting transformation.

One of the foundational pieces of NLP is the NLP Communication Model, developed by Dr. Heidi Heron and Laureli Blythe of NLP Worldwide. This model explains how we experience, filter, and act on the world around us. Understanding this process isn't just enlightening; it's empowering. With this knowledge, you can start to consciously change the way you respond to situations, behaviours, and, most importantly, anxiety.

The NLP Communication Model: How You Process an Experience

I'll never forget the moment Dr Heidi Heron, co-founder of NLP Worldwide, introduced the NLP Communication Model during my training in Sydney. It was a lightbulb moment—suddenly, I understood what was happening in my mind. My brain wasn't broken, and my anxious behaviours weren't flaws; they were responses shaped by a process I could learn to work with.

Here's how it works:

Reticular Activating System (RAS)

Have you ever noticed that once you decide on a specific car to buy, you start seeing that car everywhere? Or if you're thinking about starting a family, suddenly you see pregnant women around every corner. Those cars and baby bumps were always there, but your brain hadn't flagged them as "important" until you gave it the signal. That's your Reticular Activating System (RAS) at work—the part of your brain that acts as a filter, highlighting the things you're subconsciously focused on.

Now, think about how this applies to anxiety. If you believe, "It's so hard to find a job," your RAS will find all the evidence to support that belief, like a radar honing in on unemployment stats or rejections, reinforcing your perspective. But if you shift your belief to, "My perfect job is out there waiting for me," your RAS will start spotting opportunities you hadn't noticed before. It's all about what your mind is programmed to look for.

Filters

Your brain processes an overwhelming amount of information every second—far more than it can handle consciously. So, it uses filters—your values, beliefs, and past experiences—to sort out what's important. Without these filters, you'd be flooded by billions of bits of sensory data.

One of the most powerful filters is your beliefs. They shape what you see and how you interpret the world. For example, if you believe the world is a scary place, your brain will naturally focus on anything that supports that belief, deleting information that doesn't fit.

Distort, Delete, and Generalise

Once filtered, your mind distorts, deletes, and generalises information to create a cohesive picture. If you believe you'll fail, your mind distorts incoming information to make failure seem inevitable, deletes any evidence to the contrary, and generalises this belief across different situations. This process often creates the stories we tell ourselves, which then shape our behaviours.

The Movies in Your Mind

We constantly create mental movies of what might happen. And once that "movie" is playing, it feels so real that we emotionally react to it. Think about when you rehearse a conversation in your head, anticipating the worst. It's as if the event has already happened, triggering anxiety, fear, or anger. This emotional reaction draws us deeper into that imagined state.

States We Enter

Your emotional response creates a state—whether it's anxiety, overwhelm, or frustration—and that state leads to physical changes in the body.

Physiological Changes

When you enter an anxious state, your body responds physically. Your heart races, your stomach tightens, and your breathing becomes shallow. These physiological changes then amplify your feelings of anxiety, creating a feedback loop.

Behaviours

Finally, this process leads to behaviour, the outward expression of everything that's been happening internally. You might leave a social event, send a reactive text, or snap at someone. Yet, too often, we focus only on trying to change the behaviour without understanding the entire chain of events that led there.

When I learned this, it felt like I'd been handed a roadmap to my mind. It wasn't just about trying to stop a behaviour—it was about understanding what was driving it in the first place.

You Are Not Your Behaviours

And here's the empowering truth: you are not defined by your behaviours. In NLP, we embrace the idea that behaviours are not an expression of who you are, but rather a reflection of your current state or belief. Anxiety, for example, may influence the way you react to situations, but it is not a fixed part of your identity. You are not "an anxious person"—you are a person who experiences anxiety. This distinction frees you to explore your behaviours without attaching them to your core self. It allows for growth, change, and the realisation that you can evolve beyond any pattern you may have developed.

When you understand that your behaviours stem from a series of unconscious programs, you gain the freedom to make different choices. You can experience anxiety without letting it define your story. And now, with a clear view of the steps your mind takes before any behaviour unfolds, you can start creating meaningful changes—beginning at the belief level.

Reflective Exercise: Applying the NLP Communication Model to Your Anxiety

Let's go deeper with the NLP Communication Model. Think of a recent moment when you felt anxiety begin to rise. This exercise will help you break down the process and see how each step contributes to the final behaviour. Reflect on the following steps:

1. **Belief:** What belief surfaced during this moment?

    *   *Examples: "I'm not good enough," "Something bad is going to happen," "People will judge me."*

2. **Filtering:** How did your mind interpret or filter this experience?

    *   *Did it focus on specific details, distort information, or delete anything that didn't fit your belief?*

3. **Mental Movie:** Visualise the "movie" your mind created. What did you imagine would happen?

    *   *Were you anticipating rejection, failure, or embarrassment?*

4. **State:** How did this imagined scenario affect your emotional state?

   - *Did you feel fearful, overwhelmed, frustrated, or something else?*

5. **Physical Response**: Notice how your body responded to this state.

   - *Did your heart rate increase, or did you experience tension, sweating, or shallow breathing?*

6. **Behaviour:** Finally, consider the action you took in response.

   - *Did you avoid the situation, engage in self-criticism, or act defensively?*

Write down your responses to each of these steps. Seeing the full process mapped out can bring clarity and a greater sense of control. Recognising this progression from belief to behaviour can remind you that at any point in this chain, you have the ability to pause, reflect, and make a new choice.

Building a New Narrative

As you reflect on these exercises, think about one small shift you'd like to make. For example, if you often assume the worst in social situations, consider choosing a new belief like, "I am safe and accepted here" or "I am capable of handling whatever happens." Remind yourself that changing your beliefs is a journey and each small step counts.

The key takeaway? Change begins with awareness. By becoming conscious of the stories you tell yourself and the beliefs that drive them, you unlock the power to reshape your life. The next chapter, *Uncovering and Reframing Your Narrative*, will guide you through deeper explorations and techniques to rewrite these stories with purpose and positivity.

CHAPTER 8

Uncovering Your Hidden Narrative

"The dark night of the soul comes just before revelation. When everything is lost, and all seems darkness, then comes the new life and all that is needed."

~ Joseph Campbell

In the previous chapter, we explored how NLP helps us understand the mind and how it processes experiences. Now, we're diving deeper into the stories we tell ourselves—the ones we may not even be consciously aware of, but that shape our entire reality.

You see, the beliefs we think we hold and the stories we tell ourselves out loud are often different from the ones running beneath the surface. These hidden narratives are the real drivers of our behaviour and feelings, particularly when it comes to anxiety. That's why it's so important to remain curious and to ask ourselves the right questions. Only then can we uncover these deep-rooted beliefs and, ultimately, change the stories that are shaping our lives.

Your Secret Story... The One You Don't Talk About at Parties

Let's be honest—most of us have stories we don't broadcast at parties or post on social media. I'm not talking about that embarrassing karaoke night or the time you accidentally sent a personal email to your entire office. No, I'm talking about the deep-seated stories that shape who we are and how we navigate the world—our hidden narratives.

These are the stories we carry quietly, like a shadowy sidekick we'd rather not introduce around. They're the beliefs we've built over the years, maybe even from childhood, to make sense of our experiences. And here's the kicker: these stories don't just sit politely in the background. They drive our decisions, influence our relationships, and steer our self-worth—all without us realising it.

Think of them like the secret script running in the background of your life's movie. You may think you're confidently ad-libbing through each scene. Still, in reality, these hidden narratives are slipping lines into your dialogue, making you question if you're really "enough" or if everyone at the party somehow knows you skipped that workout yesterday.

And here's the thing: until we acknowledge these stories, they can guide our lives without our permission. But once you uncover them? You might find they don't actually have to run the show. They're stories, not truths. And you get to decide if they're still worth keeping in the script or if it's time for a rewrite.

Client Story - *Unspoken Obligations*

Let me share with you the story of one of my clients, a middle-aged woman who arrived at our sessions calm, collected, and seemingly focused. She initially sought guidance on a decision about whether her aging parents should come to live with her and her family. On the surface, her request seemed straightforward. She believed, as many of us do, that it was her duty to care for her parents as they grew older—"the right thing to do," she said.

But as we explored further, a different picture started to emerge. I asked her about what "being there" meant when she was younger, and she shifted uncomfortably. Slowly, she opened up, sharing that her parents had adopted her and her younger sister when they were very young. She had spent much of her life feeling indebted, carrying a sense of obligation that often eclipsed her own happiness. She talked about constantly "living her life for others"—always in a caretaker role, always putting her own needs last.

When I gently asked her what she wanted, if she could set aside those obligations, she paused, looking almost surprised by the question. In a soft, almost childlike voice, she said, "I want to be free." Free from the heavy responsibilities that she'd carried for so long. Free from the idea that her life was meant to fulfil others' expectations at the expense of her own dreams and desires.

Beneath the surface-level goal of deciding on living arrangements for her parents was a deeper, hidden story. Her core belief, one she had carried silently for years, was that she would "never get to live for herself"—that her life was destined to be unfulfilling, always overshadowed by the needs of others.

This story was her hidden narrative, the one that influenced her choices and shaped her perspective on life. It was the story she didn't discuss openly, the one that perhaps she hadn't even fully acknowledged herself. But once we uncovered it, she could begin to question and reframe it.

Are You Ready to Uncover Your Own Hidden Narrative?

Have you ever stopped to think about the stories you tell yourself about your anxiety? Maybe the surface story sounds like, "I just need to manage my stress better," or "I should really get over this fear." But what if, beneath these thoughts, lies a deeper narrative? A story so entrenched that it influences how you see yourself, your potential, and the world around you?

It's time to get curious and start uncovering the story beneath the surface.

1. Identifying Your Story

When you think about your anxiety, what do you believe? Write it down—whatever first comes to mind, no matter how small it seems. Now, take it a step further. What do you believe about *that* belief? Write that down, too. You're starting to peel back the layers, and it's often in these secondary layers that we begin to glimpse the hidden narrative.

By the way, you're doing great—stay with this process.

2. Naming Your Experience

Think about how you experience anxiety. Is there a specific sensation that always seems to accompany it—like a tightness in your chest, a sense of dread, or a feeling of being "trapped"? Give this experience a name, if you can. Naming it can help you recognise it more clearly, so it doesn't blend into the background.

3. Following the Breadcrumbs Back in Time

Let's get into this a bit deeper. Take a moment to think back through your life. What events, people, or situations do you remember as sources of anxiety? It could be a difficult time at school, a major life change, or a particular relationship. Sometimes, understanding our anxiety means connecting the dots from past experiences.

To help with this, grab your journal and draw a timeline of your life from birth to the present. Along the line, note the intensity of your anxiety at different points, using a scale from 0 to 10, with 10 being the most intense. Reflect on what was happening in your life during times when anxiety spiked. Were there particular events that might have influenced your beliefs about yourself or the world?

4. Identifying the Narrative Shaping Your Life Right Now

Now, take a step back and look at the bigger picture. What patterns or beliefs do you see emerging from this exercise? What story are you telling yourself about your anxiety? Is it, "I'm always going to feel this way," or "I'm not strong enough to handle stress"? This narrative might have been shaping your life for years without you realising it.

Recognising these patterns and beliefs is essential. Often, these hidden narratives control our actions, choices, and emotions. But by identifying them, you've taken the first step toward breaking free from a story that no longer serves you.

Client Story - *Transforming a Hidden Narrative*

One client I worked with—a successful high-tech executive who seemed confident and composed—came to me because she felt trapped by her intense anxiety around public speaking. On the surface, her story was that she "just needed to get over the fear." But as we dug deeper, we uncovered a more complex narrative. She realised that her anxiety stemmed from a core belief she'd carried since childhood: "If I make a mistake, people won't respect me."

Growing up, she was often pressured to excel and felt her worth was tied to her accomplishments. This belief followed her into adulthood, fueling her anxiety every time she was asked to present in front of others. By identifying and questioning this hidden narrative, she began to shift her perspective—she started to see herself as valuable regardless of any minor mistakes.

By uncovering the story behind her anxiety, she could finally work on transforming it into something empowering rather than something that held her back.

Reflective Exercise: Uncovering Your Hidden Narrative

Let's put this into practice. Take a few minutes to work through the following questions in your journal:

- **Write down a specific anxious thought or belief you have.** For example, "I'm going to mess this up."

- **Ask yourself:** What do I believe about this belief? Maybe you find a deeper belief like, "If I mess up, I'll be judged."

- **Write down the feelings that come with this belief.** What sensations arise in your body? Is it tightness, a racing heart, or a sinking feeling?

- **Reflect on your timeline.** What past experiences or influences might have contributed to this belief?

- **Ask yourself:** What is the core story I've been telling myself about my anxiety?

By working through these steps, you're beginning to see your beliefs as separate from your feelings and behaviours. This process helps you distance yourself from the narrative that has been shaping your life, creating the space to question and even rewrite that story.

Ready for the Next Step?

Uncovering these hidden narratives is an act of self-compassion and self-discovery. You're learning to question beliefs you may have held for years, and that's powerful work. In the next chapter, we'll go even deeper into how to start rewriting these stories, transforming limiting beliefs into ones that support you. There's a whole new perspective waiting to unfold, one where you're empowered to create a story that reflects who you truly are.

Ready to move on? Let's go!

CHAPTER 9

Reframe and Anchor: Building New Pathways to Empowerment

"The most fundamental aggression to ourselves, the most fundamental harm we can do to ourselves, is to remain ignorant by not having the courage and the respect to look at ourselves honestly and gently."

~ Pema Chödrön

It's time to put your RAS (Reticular Activating System) and unconscious mind to work. So, let me ask you: *What do you want to believe about your anxiety?*

In my hometown of Singleton, a family recently won a $100 million lottery jackpot. My first thought? *"It's getting closer."* I couldn't help but smile at how naturally my unconscious mind had reframed this news into something positive and hopeful.

Of course, I could have thought, *"Why couldn't that be me?"* But that would have likely led to feelings of jealousy, disappointment, or maybe even frustration. Instead, I felt uplifted, energised by the possibility that good fortune was, in some way, on its way to me.

Later that day, my youngest son came home, and I casually mentioned the news. *"Did you hear someone in Singleton won the Powerball?"* I asked. Without missing a beat, he replied, *"Yes, Mum—it's getting closer!"* I couldn't help but laugh. Reframing is powerful—and yes, it's contagious.

Each time you think or say, "I am too tired," "I don't know enough," "I'm not confident enough," or "I'll just embarrass myself," you're feeding your unconscious mind a program. The good news is that you can also choose to program it with thoughts that move you toward what you want.

Louise L. Hay once said, *"We are all doing the very best we can with the knowledge and understanding we have in the moment."* This aligns with an NLP presupposition: *"Everyone is doing the best they can with the knowledge and resources they have available."*

So, first things first: *Know that you are doing the best you can right now.* Yes, the best you can—and that's good enough. Just by reading this, you're gathering new tools and knowledge. And when you know better, you do better!

Reframing starts simply with your current thoughts. So, let's dive in and get to reframing.

Anchoring: How Your Mind Links Emotions to Memories

Now that we've explored reframing, let's look at how your unconscious mind links memories to emotions—through a concept called anchoring. Anchoring is one of the reasons reframing can be so effective, and we'll use it to support your healing journey.

Have you ever noticed how a certain smell can instantly bring back a memory? Maybe it's the scent of freshly cut grass, the warmth of baking bread, or someone's perfume as they pass by. These experiences can trigger vivid memories and feelings. That's positive anchoring, and it's something we all experience.

For me, the smell of freshly cut lawns brings me back to lazy afternoons on the verandah with my dolls while Mum mowed the lawn. She'd keep me there to watch over me as she worked around the yard. Similarly, the scent of vanilla takes me to our kitchen, where my mum baked cakes from scratch. I remember the joy of licking the raw cake mix from the bowl—a simple pleasure we seem to have lost today with all the raw egg warnings!

Anchoring isn't always positive, though. Just as pleasant memories can trigger warm feelings, unpleasant ones can evoke negative reactions. For years, the smell of crystallised ginger brought up a feeling of intense disgust in me. As a child, my nephew had once played a prank, forcing me to eat it, and ever since, just the smell was enough to make me recoil. While I still avoid crystallised ginger, I've worked through that negative anchor, and now I enjoy using ginger in my cooking.

Anchoring shows how memories and emotions are linked, whether the connection is positive or negative. It reminds us that we can work with these connections—strengthening positive anchors and reworking the negative ones—to help shift our experience of anxiety.

Anchoring Anxiety: Turning Triggers into Tools

Anxiety has a way of getting tangled up in everyday moments. Certain smells, places, sounds, or even times of day can pull us right back into the stress and tension of past experiences, hitting those anxiety buttons without warning. These triggers—anchors—are deeply tied to memories and emotions, and once they're set off, they can bring back those anxious feelings in an instant.

Here's the upside: just as we can change our thoughts, we can reset these triggers. We can create fresh, positive anchors that remind us of calm, strength, and confidence. With a little practice, these new anchors can become reliable touchstones that steer us away from anxiety and toward feeling grounded.

Exercise: Anchoring Your Thoughts for Change

Let's get into it. Start by grabbing a notebook or journal and turning to a clean page. Draw a line down the center. At the top of the left column, write **Current Thoughts.** Answer these questions honestly:

- *"When I think about my anxiety, what comes to mind?"*
- *"When I think about my anxiety, what do I feel?"*
- *"What happens next?"*

Some answers might feel neutral or even encouraging—those are fine as they are. But for any beliefs, feelings, or reactions you'd like to shift, let's look at the right column. Label it **New Thoughts** and ask yourself this simple question:

- *"If I could replace this belief or feeling with something better, what would it be?"*

Write what you *want* to believe and feel about your anxiety—perhaps, for the first time, you're seeing your thoughts as something you can shape and guide. This shift from "what I don't want" to "what I do want" is huge. Instead of focusing on the things that weigh you down, you're giving your mind a new path to follow.

Anchoring Exercise: Creating Positive Triggers

Now, let's take this further by turning these new thoughts into anchors that you can use anytime you need them. Here's how to set it up:

1. **Choose a New Thought:** Pick one of the positive beliefs from your **New Thoughts** column. Close your eyes and say this thought out loud. Picture a moment when you felt this way naturally—maybe you felt peaceful, confident, steady, or clear.

2. **Feel It in Your Body:** Let yourself feel the sensation of that memory. Did it make you stand taller, breathe a little easier, or feel a bit lighter? Picture yourself as you were in that moment, moving with ease and self-assurance.

3. **Create a Physical Anchor:** As you hold this image and feeling, press your thumb and index finger together (or choose another small gesture that feels natural). Breathe deeply and let yourself soak in the feeling as much as possible. When the feeling is at its strongest, release your fingers and open your eyes.

4. **Make it a Habit:** Use this anchoring gesture whenever you want to reconnect with that feeling. Over time, the simple act of pressing your fingers together will start to trigger that positive emotion, giving you a reliable anchor for steadying yourself whenever you need it.

By repeating this anchor, you're creating new mental pathways. You're not only reshaping your thoughts, you're building a reliable way to bring yourself back to what matters. You're shifting from reacting to anxiety to choosing how you want to feel.

Moving Forward

With these exercises, you're taking real steps toward reshaping the way you think and feel. Each time you set a new anchor, you're replacing old reactions with choices that serve you better. You're training your brain to expect positive cues and building a new outlook, one thought at a time.

Take a moment to recognise how far you've come. This isn't about finding the "right" way to handle anxiety; it's about trying something different and giving yourself options. With each step, you're creating a foundation that can support you, whatever comes your way. I'm excited to see what you uncover next as we keep moving forward together.

CHAPTER 10

Thoughts as Beliefs: The Hidden Power of Everyday Thinking

"You are loved and important, and you bring to this world things that no one else can."

~ The Boy, The Mole, The Fox and The Horse Movie

In the last chapter, we explored the concept of anchoring—how our thoughts, beliefs, and memories can leave lasting imprints on us, often without our awareness. Now, let's dive deeper into something that may sound simple but has an enormous impact: understanding the difference between a thought and a belief. Because when we leave our thoughts unchecked, they can grow into powerful narratives that shape our behaviours, emotions, and, ultimately, our experiences.

The Difference Between a Thought and a Belief

Every day, we have thousands of thoughts—some big, some small, some fleeting, and others that linger. But have you ever paused to think about what a thought really is? Is it just a passing idea, a spark of insight, a momentary opinion, or perhaps an observation? Or is it something more? And if so, at what point does a thought turn into something deeper, something that influences you?

And here's an even more intriguing question: If I think something, does that mean I actually believe it?

Picture your thoughts as bubbles floating in your mind. Some of these bubbles pop up and disappear in an instant—maybe a stray idea like "I'd love a coffee right now." Others, however, stick around, replaying in your mind, picking up emotional weight. The more a thought lingers and repeats, gathering significance, the more likely it is to evolve into a belief.

When Anxiety Turns Thoughts into Beliefs

For anyone dealing with anxiety, it often feels like those bubbles multiply, filling up every corner of your mind and making it hard to see past them. Anxiety doesn't just increase the volume of thoughts you have—it amplifies them, making fleeting concerns feel lasting, turning momentary worries into deeply ingrained beliefs. Without even realising it, worries, fears, and doubts can go from being just thoughts to becoming solid beliefs.

When a thought becomes a belief, it acts like a filter through which you see the world. An anxious thought like "What if I can't handle this?" transforms into a belief that colours every action, decision, and interaction. Suddenly, it's not just a worry; it's a way you start seeing yourself—a narrative that becomes part of who you are.

Frozen in Fear or Excited Butterflies? How Thoughts and Beliefs Impact the Body

Every thought has the potential to evoke a physical reaction, and sometimes, that reaction is immediate. Other times, it builds up over days, weeks, or even years, gaining momentum until it affects us deeply. Louise Hay once described anxiety as "not trusting the flow and process of life." That hits close to home for so many of us. So here's a question to consider: When did you stop trusting the flow of life? Can you recall a specific time or event?

Client Story - *Thoughts, Beliefs, and the Body's Reactions*

One of my clients, let's call him Tom, once shared a story with me that captures this process perfectly. Tom had been struggling with debilitating migraines for years. These migraines weren't just painful; they robbed him of his weekends, his downtime, and the chance to engage in the hobbies he loved. He'd tell me that they always hit just when he was finally free from work, just as he was looking forward to doing something for himself. Even a beloved hobby, like working on his car, would be disrupted by these headaches.

"What do you believe about the end of the workweek?" I asked him one day.

He thought about it, then replied, "I believe it's finally my time to do what I want." I pressed a little further. "What do you mean by 'finally'?" I asked.

"Well," he explained, "I've been working hard all week. Now it's time to relax and enjoy myself."

And here's where it got interesting. His thoughts—and, more importantly, his beliefs—were actively shaping his experience. Tom's unconscious mind, interpreting these beliefs literally, was preparing his body for rest and recovery, not for engaging in hands-on hobbies. By the time he got home, his body was already in "rest mode," and that's when his migraines would kick in, forcing him to lie down. Although it was frustrating for him, the migraine served a purpose: it provided the rest he'd been unconsciously telling himself he needed.

Through this process, Tom's belief about needing rest didn't just remain an idea; it became a physical reality. His unconscious mind filtered his thoughts and created a mental movie of exhaustion, and his body responded accordingly. The result? A migraine that enforced the "rest" his mind had anchored to his weekends.

Revisiting the NLP Communication Model: When Thoughts Become Reality

To see just how powerful a simple belief can be, let's break down Tom's experience using the NLP Communication Model. This model shows us that our beliefs don't just live in our minds; they shape how we experience reality, often in ways we don't fully realise.

For Tom, the belief "I've worked hard all week, and I'm really tired" sets off a whole sequence of events in his mind and body. Here's how it unfolds:

First, his Reticular Activating System (RAS) gets to work. The RAS is like an internal radar, filtering and highlighting anything that supports Tom's belief that he's exhausted. So, by the time he's driving home, his RAS has filtered out anything that might contradict his tiredness. Instead, it's tuning in to every little sign of fatigue—the weight of his eyelids, the tension in his shoulders, the mental rundown of his week's workload.

With this belief as his filter, Tom starts running a mental movie in his head. He sees himself trudging into the garage, feeling too drained to find his tools, struggling to enjoy the very thing he'd been looking forward to all week. This mental movie plays out in vivid detail, becoming more real with each replay. And with every replay, his body buys into it more and more.

Here's where the magic—or the mischief—of the mind kicks in. The more Tom plays this movie in his head, the more his body responds as if it's actually happening. His energy dips, his enthusiasm fades, and a sense of weariness settles in. By the time he arrives home, his body has already gone into shutdown mode, sending him straight to bed. And, like clockwork, a migraine sets in, enforcing the rest he's unconsciously craving.

What's fascinating here is that Tom's migraine, as frustrating as it is, serves a purpose. In NLP, we often say that every behaviour has a positive intention. Tom's body, through the migraine, is saying, "You need rest, and I'm making sure you get it." His unconscious mind has turned this belief into a physical experience, ensuring he gets the rest he believes he needs.

The Power of Beliefs: How They Shape Our Reality

Tom's story brings us to a powerful truth: our beliefs create our experiences. We tend to think of beliefs as thoughts that stay locked in our heads, but they're much more than that. They shape the world we see and how we respond to it. When you deeply believe something—whether it's "I'm exhausted" or "I'm not good enough"—your RAS goes to work, finding all the evidence to back up that belief, almost as if it's on a mission to prove you right.

This is why it's so crucial to become aware of what you believe, especially if those beliefs aren't helping you. Think about it: if you're always telling yourself, "I'm too anxious," your RAS will zero in on situations that amplify that anxiety, reinforcing the belief and creating a cycle that keeps you stuck. But here's the silver lining: what if we flipped that belief? What if, instead of "I'm too anxious," we chose to feed our minds a different story, like "I'm ready to face the day"?

When you shift your beliefs, you start changing the story your mind is telling you. As your mind adopts a new story, it begins to find evidence for that story, gradually transforming your experience from the inside out.

Practical Reflection: Changing Your Thoughts to Change Your Reality

Let's take a closer look at the beliefs you hold about your anxiety and the way they shape your everyday experience. This isn't about "fixing" anything just yet—just about understanding how your mind is currently working. Find a quiet space, and when you're ready, work through these questions:

1. Naming Your Core Beliefs

What do you believe about your anxiety? Write down the first few things that come to mind. Maybe it's "My anxiety is just part of who I am" or "I don't have control over this." Whatever it is, jot it down without judgment.

2. Observing the Thoughts Linked to These Beliefs

Now, consider the thoughts that frequently pop up around these beliefs. For example, if you believe "I'll always be this way," you might notice thoughts like, "I'm not as capable as others" or "I wish I could just get over this." Write down these recurring thoughts and notice any patterns.

3. Identifying How These Thoughts Shape Your Day-to-Day

Reflect on how these thoughts and beliefs influence your everyday life. How do they impact your mood, your interactions, or your decisions? Are they creating a feeling of being stuck or limited? Write down any ways these beliefs seem to affect your reality, even in small ways.

4. Imagining a Different Narrative

Imagine for a moment: If you could loosen the grip of one of these beliefs, how might that change things for you? If "I'll always be this way" *wasn't* true, what possibilities might open up? You don't need to fully believe this alternative yet—just allow yourself to consider it.

A Path Forward

Realising your beliefs and how they shape your experience is an empowering step. Just by noticing these patterns, you're already creating a bit of room for change. It might feel small at first, but this space is where transformation begins.

With the tools of NLP, you'll have the ability to go beyond just recognising your patterns. You'll be equipped to reshape the stories that might have felt unchangeable, turning them into ones that truly serve you. Imagine guiding your mind to create a reality that's in line with your goals, values, and the kind of life you genuinely want to live. This isn't just abstract theory or wishful thinking—it's the start of living a life designed by choice rather than by autopilot.

Remember, it all starts with a single thought—a small step that, when repeated, gains momentum. As you continue, you'll find these new ways of thinking and feeling becoming natural, even easy. Each of these steps brings you closer to a life that feels not only manageable but meaningful, purposeful, and yours.

So, as you finish this section, take a moment to acknowledge how far you've already come. Recognising these patterns, reflecting on them, and even imagining new possibilities are powerful first steps. The best part? You're just getting started.

CHAPTER 11

How the Past Has Shaped Your Future

"The wound is the place where the light enters you."

~ Rumi

In the last chapter, we took some important first steps. We began to reframe your thoughts and shift your Reticular Activating System (RAS) toward what you truly want—calm, peace, and freedom from anxiety. And I hope you can already feel it—the subtle, gentle shift in how you experience life. Like a soft breeze nudging you forward, you're making progress. And you can sense it, can't you?

Now, we're going to take our journey a little deeper. This chapter is all about understanding the origins of your anxiety and exploring how past experiences, traumas, and beliefs may still be influencing how you see the world today. Together, we'll look at where these roots may have begun to take hold so that we can start to loosen and heal them.

Exploring the Impact of Past Events on Present Beliefs

Anxiety is rarely just about what's happening in the moment. Often, it's a response shaped by echoes from past experiences. Events from childhood or adolescence, no matter how big or small, have a way of sticking with us. They can create beliefs about ourselves or the world that influence how we respond, sometimes in ways we don't even realise.

For many of us, anxiety is tied to certain deeply held beliefs—about not being good enough, about needing to please others to feel safe, or about constantly preparing for the worst. These beliefs didn't just appear overnight; they were formed gradually, often in response to experiences we had when we were young and impressionable.

Take a moment to reflect: can you think of any memories from your past that might have contributed to the way you feel about yourself or the world today? Are there experiences that could be connected to your feelings of worry, self-doubt, or the need to be constantly "on guard"? You don't have to dive too deep yet, just notice what comes up. Sometimes, awareness alone is a powerful first step.

My Story - *A Turning Point from Childhood*

Let me share a story from my own life, one that had a lasting impact on me. When I was around 11 years old, I felt completely out of place. Friendships at school were tough, and I struggled to find where I belonged. My foster mum, who had been with me since I was a baby, was my safe haven. But at that time, I was overwhelmed, and I thought a change would make things better.

So, in what felt like a bold move, I asked my foster mum if I could go live with my biological mum. Looking back, I realise it was my first attempt at "running away" from my challenges, though I didn't understand it fully at the time. I'll never forget how painful it was—one of the hardest moments of my life.

My foster mum cried but told me she'd support my choice if it were what I truly wanted. I remember feeling this deep, sick feeling like I'd broken something between us. When I called my biological mum, she said it wasn't a good idea. Suddenly, I felt abandoned by her as well. I thought I'd made an irreversible mistake, leaving me feeling utterly alone.

Thankfully, my foster mum was there to sweep me back into her arms with the same unconditional love as always. But that moment shaped something deep within me. I started feeling like I always had to meet others' expectations, becoming a "people pleaser" to avoid the risk of being abandoned again. This tendency to people-please became one of the roots of my anxiety.

ACE - The Silent Architect of Anxiety

Have you heard of the Adverse Childhood Experiences (ACE) study? This study, which began in 1997, revealed how early experiences in life can influence mental health, sometimes shaping it in powerful ways. The study showed that when someone has several ACEs, they're more likely to experience patterns of persistent worry, anxiety, or hypervigilance later on. Even if we don't consciously remember these experiences, they can silently shape the foundation of our anxiety.

But here's something important to remember:

You are not your trauma.

You may have gone through difficult or even painful experiences, but those moments don't define you. As trauma expert Gabor Maté puts it, *trauma isn't about what happened to you—it's about what happened inside you as a result.* In other words, your anxiety isn't who you are. It's a response, a coping mechanism, often rooted in those early wounds.

One of my clients once said, "I am not the problem. It's the wound that's the problem." And that is exactly right. *You* are not the problem— your anxiety is the result of a wound that now needs compassion and healing.

Big T & Little T Trauma

The word "trauma" comes up often these days, which is good because it opens up space for conversations we might not have had before. But sometimes, it can lead people to dismiss their struggles. I often hear people say, "I didn't have any trauma. I had a great childhood," or "I don't have anything big to complain about."

Here's the thing: trauma doesn't always look like we think it should. There's what we call "Big T Trauma"—the kind we associate with major life events like abuse, neglect, or loss. And then there's "Little T Trauma"—those smaller but impactful moments, like feeling ignored, shamed, or rejected in childhood. Both types matter. Both can leave lasting marks.

Maybe you remember moments that seem minor now but felt intense when you were young. Perhaps you were left alone to cry, or you felt shamed for wanting something. These experiences might seem trivial, but they can create feelings of fear or unworthiness that linger long into adulthood.

Take a moment to consider your own experiences. Are there any memories, big or small, that might have shaped how you relate to the world? Don't worry if you're unsure; just gently allow yourself to notice what comes up. Recognising these experiences isn't about placing blame—it's about understanding the full picture of who you are.

Reflective Exercise - Mapping Your Timeline

One way to explore these influences is by mapping your personal timeline. Each of us carries a unique timeline, a series of events that have shaped who we are today. Some moments are vivid, while others may be barely conscious, but they all leave an imprint.

Let's try this simple exercise together:

1. **Close your eyes for a moment.** Think about a memory, perhaps something recent. Notice where that memory seems to "appear" in your mind. Does it feel like it's to your left? Behind you? Just observe.

2. **Now, imagine where you "see" your future.** Is it in front of you? Off to the side? Notice where it feels, without judging.

3. **With your eyes still closed, picture your entire timeline.** Visualise your past memories and future aspirations as they align around you. Is there a pattern? Does one side feel heavier or lighter? Just notice.

When you're ready, open your eyes and draw this timeline in your journal. Label your past, your future and the present. Mark significant moments in your past that come to mind. Think about events that may have shaped the way you respond to the world. Moments that caused you concern, where you felt embarrassed, lost, ashamed? There's no need to analyse too deeply—just allow any memories or insights to flow naturally.

Remember, this is the "Learning" phase of the CALM model. By bringing awareness to where your anxiety might come from, you're starting to shift your relationship with it. Keep this timeline close; it will serve as a gentle guide as we move forward.

From the Past to the Future

As you reflect on the timeline of your life and those moments, big or small, that have shaped you, remember that each memory and belief you uncover brings you one step closer to understanding the roots of your anxiety. This exploration is about recognising—not judging—how these early experiences have influenced your present feelings.

So now that you've taken a deeper look at the past, I invite you to think about the future. What if you could begin to rewrite these patterns? What if you could create a mental picture of your life without anxiety, one where calm, confidence, and joy guide your experience? In the next chapter, we'll explore how you can do just that—by tapping into the power of your mind to envision a new way forward, one that moves you closer to the life you truly want.

CHAPTER 12

Rewiring for Calm - Envisioning Your Anxiety-Free Future

"If we observe ourselves truthfully and non-judgmentally, seeing the mechanisms of our personality in action, we can wake up, and our lives can be a miraculous unfolding of beauty and joy."

~ Don Richard Riso

As you've learned, much of our anxiety is rooted in the stories we tell ourselves. These stories are often filled with worry, fear, and endless "what ifs." But just as your mind can create a future clouded by anxiety, it can also create a future filled with peace, joy, and calm. And this isn't just wishful thinking—it's a powerful mental process that can reshape how you think and feel in the present.

Imagine this: every time you vividly picture yourself free from anxiety, your brain activates a network called the default mode network (DMN). This network includes areas like the hippocampus, which holds our memories, and the prefrontal cortex, which helps with planning and decision-making. When these parts of your brain light up, they don't just daydream—they actively construct a mental picture of a calm, anxiety-free future. Think of it like mental rehearsal; your brain is getting ready for a new reality.

So, let's take a moment here. Reflect on the stories you currently tell yourself when you feel anxious. Do they focus on things that might go wrong? Are they full of unknowns? Write down a few of these anxious stories. Now, ask yourself: what could be the opposite of each story? For example, if your mind says, "What if I mess up?" try flipping it to, "What if I handle this smoothly?" Write down each counter-story beside the original ones. This is a first step in teaching your mind to imagine possibilities beyond anxiety."

How the Brain Rewires Through Imagination

Here's where the magic of visualisation truly takes shape. When you imagine a future where anxiety doesn't control you, you're doing more than creating a hopeful picture. You're actively engaging your brain's emotional centres, allowing you to feel calm, peaceful, and in control—

even if just for a moment. Each time you practice this, you're training your brain to experience these feelings more naturally, even in real-life situations.

The science behind it is fascinating. Each time you visualise yourself as calm and confident, your brain is forming new neural pathways, like well-trodden trails in a forest. The more you "walk" these trails by revisiting your vision of calm, the stronger they become. Over time, this mental map for calm responses becomes easier to access, especially during moments that might have once triggered anxiety.

Let's try a quick exercise. Think about a moment in your life when you've experienced calm. It could be as simple as sitting with a cup of tea, walking in nature, or a time you felt completely at ease. Bring this memory to mind and focus on the feelings it created. Where do you feel this calmness in your body? Is it a warmth in your chest? A lightness in your shoulders? Take a few minutes to fully immerse yourself in this memory. This process strengthens your ability to recall and recreate these feelings in new situations."

Reflective Exercise - Reimagining Your Future Self

Now, let's build on these ideas with an exercise that will help you imagine your future self, free from anxiety. This exercise is meant to bring you closer to the reality you're working toward by helping you feel, see, and embody the calm you desire.

1. **Close your eyes and take a few deep breaths.** With each breath, let go of any tension you feel. Notice if any resistance comes up as you try to imagine yourself anxiety-free. Just observe it and let it pass.

2. **Imagine yourself in a future moment.** In this vision, you've fully overcome your anxiety. Picture yourself moving through your day. Notice your posture, your expressions, and the way you interact with others. What do you feel in this anxiety-free state? Do you feel relaxed, confident, happy, and at ease? Write down any emotions or physical sensations that arise.

3. **Visualise how you carry yourself.** Are you standing a bit taller? Moving more freely? Breathing more naturally? Picture yourself moving through daily activities with ease. Pay attention to the posture, the tone of your voice, and the lightness in your body. Try to hear the words you are saying if you're speaking to someone.

4. **Tune in to your body.** Where do you feel this relaxed happiness in your body? Maybe you notice a sense of warmth, a pleasant lightness, or a feeling of groundedness in your core. Visualise that feeling growing and spreading through you, replacing any tightness or tension that anxiety used to create.

5. **Reflect on your thoughts.** What are you thinking in this future state? How have your thoughts shifted? Maybe they're more compassionate, hopeful, or clear. Let yourself imagine the kinds of thoughts that flow through your mind when you're living without anxiety.

When you finish, open your eyes and reflect. How did it feel to imagine this version of yourself? Write down anything that stood out to you during the exercise. Remember, this vision of yourself is entirely within reach. Practising this future pacing helps reinforce the calm, ease, and confidence you're creating for yourself.

▌My Story - *Parenting and Compassion*

I'll never forget the early days of being a mother, trying to follow all the expert advice. I was told that I needed to teach my son to 'self-soothe,' which meant leaving him to cry in his crib. I remember sitting outside his room, listening to his cries. It was agonising for both of us. Eventually, I couldn't bear it any longer—I went in, picked him up, and he clung to me like his heart was breaking.

At the time, I thought I was doing the right thing by following those "rules." But over the years, I came to realise that there's so much power in simply showing up with compassion, whether for a child, a loved one, or ourselves. Sometimes, our best healing comes when we trust our instincts and respond with empathy instead of rigid rules.

This reflection is important because just as I had to learn to trust my instincts as a parent, rewiring anxiety also involves learning to trust yourself. The practice of self-compassion is like creating a safe space within yourself, where anxiety has less of a hold.

Take a few minutes to write a letter to yourself as if you were a dear friend or a loving parent. What words of reassurance and understanding would you offer yourself? Remind yourself that, like any other person, you're allowed patience, understanding, and compassion. Practising this kindness toward yourself each day will reinforce a new, gentler story in place of anxiety."

Final Thoughts on Embracing a New Story

As you complete this chapter, please take a moment to reflect on what it feels like to imagine a future free from anxiety. You've done powerful work here, from recognising the past to envisioning a new way forward. Each time you practice this visualisation, you're creating a new path, one that brings you closer to a life where peace, confidence, and calm guide your days.

Consider what story you'd like to carry with you now. The stories we tell ourselves can be potent—so as you move forward, try to replace any old, limiting narratives with empowering ones. A helpful reminder might be: 'I am in the process of building my calm, and I am worthy of peace.' Repeat it to yourself whenever doubt creeps in. With each step, you're moving closer to a life that is centred in the calm you've worked so hard to create.

Remember, as we move into the final chapters, that the vision you're creating isn't just a dream. It's the reality you're building—one step, one story, and one moment of calm at a time.

CHAPTER 13

Creating a New Path Forward

"The meaning of life is just to be alive. It is so plain and so obvious and so simple. And yet, everybody rushes around in a great panic as if it were necessary to achieve something beyond themselves."

~ Alan Watts

Every meaningful change starts with a moment of clarity. Sometimes, we get so caught up in what we *don't* want that we forget to ask ourselves the simplest, most powerful question: "What do I truly want?" In this chapter, we'll uncover how shifting our focus from fear to desire can create a path toward peace and fulfilment, beginning with one woman's journey to rediscover what she's really searching for.

Client Story - *The Power of Getting Clear on What You Want*

A tearful woman appears on my screen. Thousands of miles separate us, yet her sorrow feels so close, almost tangible. She opens up about the pain of her divorce and the deeper ache of feeling shut out by her adult children. Her texts go unanswered, leaving her heart stinging with rejection. As she shares her story, I can feel the weight of her hurt.

When she finally pauses, I ask her gently, "What do you want?"

At first, her answer is all about what she *doesn't* want: "I don't want to be the one initiating everything," "I don't want to feel rejected," "I don't want to be blamed or ignored."

But as I guide her back to the question, "What do you *really* want?" her voice softens.

"I want to feel calm," she says. "At peace with my decisions. I want to feel OK just as I am."

And that's the key.

NLP Presupposition: Where Your Focus Goes, Your Energy Flows

When we focus on what we *don't* want, our energy tends to gravitate toward those things. We worry, we overthink, and our minds search for evidence to support our fears. But shifting our focus to what we do want changes everything. Our minds start seeing possibilities, solutions, and openings.

This shift in focus is powerful. It gives your Reticular Activating System (RAS) a new directive, prompting your brain to search for things that align with your desired state. And as you'll see, the more you focus on what you want, the more your energy naturally moves in that direction.

Defining What You Want

Let's dig into defining what you *really* want.

Imagine shedding the layers of anxiety, overthinking, and fear. Who would you like to be instead? What does your ideal emotional state look like? How would you like to move through life?

Picture those moments when anxiety used to take over—now replaced with calm. How would you prefer to respond in situations that once triggered you? How would you want to feel when facing uncertainty or judgment from others?

- What do you want to feel?

- What do you want to think?

- What do you want to see in yourself?

- What do you want to hear from your inner voice?

Take a few moments to write this down. Let yourself dream a little. This is your time to get specific, so don't hold back—allow the words to flow freely.

The Real Reason You Want to Let Go of Anxiety

Congratulations! You've identified your desired state. Please take a moment to feel what it's like to imagine yourself living this way. It feels good, doesn't it? Picture yourself embodying this new way of being: what are you doing, where are you, and how does it feel?

Now, ask yourself: *For what purpose do I want to be this way?*

Here's where it gets interesting—the reason you want to feel calm, confident, and anxiety-free may actually be connected to your current state of anxiety.

Let me explain.

NLP Presupposition: Every Behaviour Has a Positive Intention

One of the most powerful concepts in NLP is the understanding that every behaviour, even the ones we dislike, is rooted in a positive intention. This idea applies to every anxious thought, worry, or moment of avoidance. The behaviours tied to your anxiety—overthinking, excessive planning, avoiding certain situations—are strategies your mind uses to protect you. Often, these behaviours stem from a need for safety, control, certainty, or even peace.

Think about it this way: your mind, whether consciously or not, believes that these anxious responses are serving you. By keeping you alert, preparing you for the worst, or steering you away from perceived risks, your anxiety is trying to meet a need. Sometimes, that need might be for security, reassurance, or stability. And even though it can feel uncomfortable, frustrating, or even exhausting, your anxiety is essentially trying to protect you.

For many people, recognising the positive intention behind their anxiety can be a breakthrough moment. It allows us to step back from seeing anxiety as something purely negative and begin understanding it as a message—a signal that something within us wants attention, care, or a sense of safety. Instead of feeling at odds with anxiety, this perspective allows us to shift towards acknowledging its purpose, even if we need to find healthier ways for it to meet our needs.

Client Story- *Sarah's Anxiety and the Need for Control*

Sarah was a successful project manager known for her meticulous attention to detail. She was highly valued at work, but privately, she struggled with intense anxiety that would take hold whenever a new project came up. Even though she had years of experience and a proven track record, Sarah's mind would fill with anxious thoughts: *What if I miss something important? What if my team thinks I'm not capable?*

The anxiety grew to a point where she would work long hours, triple-checking every detail. She avoided delegating tasks, feeling that she needed to oversee everything personally. Her family noticed her becoming increasingly irritable and withdrawn. Sarah found herself lying awake at night, replaying scenarios in her mind, convinced that something would go wrong if she didn't stay on top of every detail.

Through coaching, Sarah began exploring the root of her anxiety. She discovered that beneath the surface, her mind was trying to keep her safe by controlling every possible outcome. Sarah's anxiety was deeply tied to her need for security and the desire to be seen as competent. Each anxious thought was, in its way, a strategy to prevent failure and maintain control. By overworking herself, Sarah's mind was attempting to reassure her that she was prepared and capable, even though the process was exhausting.

Once Sarah realised that her anxiety had a positive intention—to protect her from feelings of inadequacy and potential criticism—she began to see her patterns with a new perspective. She recognised that her mind was trying to serve her by creating a sense of control, but she also saw how these behaviours were unsustainable and damaging her well-being.

From this point, Sarah was able to start reworking her strategies. She gradually allowed herself to delegate tasks, practised trust in her team, and learned that she could feel secure without micromanaging every detail. Her anxiety lessened as she built up her confidence, knowing she could maintain her standards without sacrificing her peace.

Reflective Questions

Now, think about your own experiences. When you feel anxious or compelled to act in certain ways, ask yourself: What is this behaviour trying to protect me from? What deeper need might my anxiety be addressing?

Is your anxiety trying to offer you safety, control, reassurance, or perhaps a sense of preparedness? By understanding the positive intention behind it, you can start to appreciate your anxiety's message and explore healthier ways to meet these needs.

Evidence: How Will You Know When You've Arrived?

To fully embrace this new path, it's essential to pinpoint the evidence that will show you've reached your desired state. How will you know when you've achieved that quiet mind, that peaceful sense of being (or whatever else you've identified as your goal)?

My Story - *Recognising Your Shift from Anxiety*

When I was a child, I remember wanting a Baby Alive doll so badly that it took over my thoughts for weeks. I imagined everything: unwrapping it, feeling the thrill in my heart, dressing it in special clothes, and even setting it by my side at Christmas dinner. I knew exactly where it would sleep, and I could see myself proudly pushing it in a little stroller. When I finally unwrapped it on Christmas morning, it was everything I'd dreamed. I could see it, feel it, hold it—and that joy in my heart was the proof that my wish had come true.

Therapeutic evidence is similar. You need a way to recognise when you've reached your desired state.

How will your thoughts, feelings, and behaviours shift when you've let go of anxiety?

Try using this template to guide you:

- *I will know I've moved beyond my anxiety because when I think of (insert scenario), I will feel (insert emotion or state).*

- *When I imagine myself in (insert situation), I will notice (insert physical sensation or behaviour).*

You've already made big strides by getting clear on what you truly want and understanding the supportive role your anxiety has been trying to play. By shifting your focus from fears to desires, you've taken some of the most important steps toward building a life where anxiety doesn't have to take centre stage. Recognising that even your anxiety has had a positive intention can be a powerful shift—it's the beginning of a more compassionate relationship with yourself. Now, with this fresh perspective, you're ready to explore how to turn these insights into lasting, everyday change.

CHAPTER 14

Aligning Head, Heart, & Gut

"When seeking guidance, don't ever listen to the tiny-hearted. Be kind to them, heap them with blessing, cajole them, but do not follow their advice."

~ Clarissa Pinkola Estes

So, now you know what you want, and you've started to see your anxiety in a new light. There's just one more piece to this puzzle. While your mind is powerful, there's more to your experience than just your thoughts. You actually have three centres of intelligence: your head, heart, and gut. When these centres work together, you make choices that feel balanced, authentic, and grounded.

In this chapter, we'll explore how to align these three centres to help you move through anxiety with calm and resilience. It's all about creating inner harmony that supports you. Ready to dive in? Let's get started.

Our Three Brains: Head, Heart, and Gut

Have you ever felt caught between what you *think* and what you *feel*? Or have you experienced a gut instinct that seems to know something before your mind does? These moments happen because we don't just have one brain—we have three centres of intelligence: the head, heart, and gut.

In NLP, these three centres are seen as essential for how we process, decide, and navigate life. I learned this concept deeply during my training with Dr. Heidi Heron at NLP Worldwide Institutes. Her wisdom in connecting these three brains has profoundly shaped my approach, and I'm incredibly grateful for the insights she shared.

Most of us rely more on one of these centres than the others, but the real power comes when we align all three—creating a balance that lets us tap into our full potential.

1. The Head Brain: The Seat of Logic and Reason

The head brain, located in the skull, is where we process logic, reasoning, and intellectual understanding. This is the part of you that plans, solves problems and organises information.

Research shows that the head brain governs conscious thinking and decision-making. It's the brain we're most familiar with, often dominating our work and problem-solving. However, relying solely on the head brain can lead to overthinking, analysis paralysis, or rationalising away emotions, leaving us feeling disconnected from our deeper wisdom.

2. The Heart Brain: The Centre of Emotions and Values

The heart is much more than a muscle pumping blood. Studies reveal that it has its own nervous system—often called the "heart brain"—which sends more signals to the brain than it receives. This means the heart plays a major role in our emotions, connections, and values.

The heart brain processes in ways tied to empathy, love, and our connections to others. When we talk about "following our heart," we're actually referring to this centre of intelligence. It guides us in relationships and situations where values and emotional truths are key.

Ignoring the wisdom of the heart can lead us to feel out of sync with what truly matters.

3. The Gut Brain: The Source of Instinct and Intuition

The gut brain, scientifically known as the enteric nervous system (ENS), is located in the digestive tract. This centre governs instinct and intuition—those "gut feelings" that arise when something feels "off." The gut often responds first, even before the head brain can analyse a situation.

The gut brain is wired to protect us and keep us safe, responding quickly without needing lengthy analysis. It's deeply connected to intuition, guiding us in those moments when we just *know* something, even if we can't explain why.

Why Aligning Your Three Brains Matters

When your head, heart, and gut are out of sync, decision-making can feel like an internal tug-of-war. You might think one thing but feel another, or your gut may pull you in a direction that your head tries to rationalise away. Each brain serves a unique purpose, and when aligned, they work together to help you make clearer, more confident decisions and feel at ease in your actions.

Through my NLP training with Dr. Heidi Heron, I learned to value this alignment deeply. She helped me understand that real transformation happens when we listen to all parts of ourselves—not just one.

Aligning with What You Want

Now that we've explored these three brains, think about how they can work together as you strive to shift your state, especially when it comes to overcoming anxiety. It's not enough to just *think* your way out of anxiety with your head. To truly embody change, you also need to connect with your heart (emotional centre) and tune into your gut (instinctual centre).

Why "Fake It Till You Make It" Is Rubbish Advice

In my early days of consulting, I was invited to speak at a local event. Living with undeclared anxiety, I was a bundle of nerves leading up to the talk. Someone offered me that all-too-common advice: *"Just fake it till you make it!"*

Determined to follow their advice, I tried to push through my dread, sickness, and fear. I ignored every signal my body was sending—the knots in my stomach, the racing thoughts keeping me up at night.

The result? I was an anxious mess on stage. I had too many slides, fumbled with my notes, and stood rigidly behind the podium, completely disconnected from the audience. My heart pounded so loudly that I could barely concentrate. A kind woman even offered to get me water (yes, my anxiety was that obvious). Once the presentation ended, I slipped out of the room as quickly as I could, feeling humiliated.

"Faking it" didn't work because I ignored every signal from my heart and gut. I was so focused on how I *thought* I should act (head brain) that I disconnected from how I actually *felt* (heart brain) and what my gut was trying to warn me about.

Faking it means suppressing the valuable messages from our body, dismissing our anxiety rather than understanding it. And no one likes to be dismissed—especially not anxiety.

NLP Presupposition: There Is No Failure, Only Feedback

If I'd acknowledged my anxiety and been real with myself, I could have learned what it was trying to tell me. Perhaps I needed more practice, a different approach, or simply a little compassion. "Fake it till you make it?" Rubbish.

I say: *Feel it to reveal it.*

Exercise: Aligning the Three Brains

Let's bring your head, heart, and gut into alignment.

Begin by taking a few deep breaths and thinking of a recent moment when you felt anxious. As you move through the next steps, let whatever comes to mind arrive naturally, observing without judgment.

1. **Head:** Start by asking your head what it thinks about the situation. What thoughts, stories, or beliefs is your mind telling you? Write these down.

2. **Heart:** Now, focus on your heart. What emotions come up around the situation? What does your heart want to express? Write down these feelings.

3. **Gut:** Finally, tune into your gut. What is your instinct saying about the situation? Do you feel safe or threatened? What is your gut urging you to do? Write that down.

Once you've written everything down, review your notes. Are your head, heart, and gut in alignment, or do they seem to pull in different directions?

Now, without writing further, close your eyes and mentally revisit the situation, moving it gently through each centre: your head, your heart, and your gut. As you filter the situation through each centre, notice what insights arise. Continue until you feel a sense of congruence—where you sense the wisdom of each centre becoming aligned with the situation. When it feels in alignment, write down what you now know and believe about it.

By listening to each of these centres, you're allowing your anxiety to be heard, felt, and understood. This process creates space for greater understanding, letting the intelligence from each of your centres contribute to the situation you're facing.

Exercise: Speaking with Your Anxiety

As you read this, take a moment to settle in. Become aware of your surroundings, and notice how you're feeling right now. Let yourself breathe slowly and deeply, and gently bring to mind a recent time when anxiety showed up for you. You don't need to relive the experience—just observe, with a soft curiosity, how anxiety makes itself known to you. Where do you usually feel it in your body? Is it in your head? Your chest? Your gut? Or maybe somewhere else?

As you continue, picture in your mind's eye what anxiety feels like. Is there a tightness, a flutter, or perhaps a heavy weight pressing down? Simply notice these sensations without judging or trying to change them. You might even imagine that anxiety has a colour, shape, or texture. Does it feel rough or smooth? Heavy or light? Let whatever comes up be completely okay.

Now, in your imagination, picture yourself gently bringing this sensation outside of your body. Visualise holding it in your hands—as unusual as that may sound, just see it there in front of you. What does it look like now that it's outside of you? Observe it with a little more curiosity and a bit of distance.

As you hold it, imagine giving this anxiety a voice, even just for a moment. It doesn't need to speak loudly—just enough to convey what it's been trying to do for you. You might ask it something like: *"What are you trying to achieve for me?"* Notice what comes to mind. Is it trying to protect you? Keep you safe? Let any answer arise gently, without forcing it. Whatever response you receive, allow it to sit with you, knowing you can return to this awareness anytime.

Next, consider letting your anxiety know that, while you appreciate its efforts, the way it's been showing up has actually made things harder for you. You might ask it: *"What do you need from me so you don't have to show up in this way?"* Be open to whatever response comes. It might surprise you how clearly your anxiety knows what it needs.

As you sit with these insights, notice the energy of your anxiety begins to shift. Maybe its colour or shape changes. Perhaps it feels a little lighter or different now that you've listened to it. Allow these shifts to unfold naturally.

Finally, imagine gently bringing this transformed anxiety back inside of you—but this time, in a way that feels softer, more integrated, and less heavy. How does it feel to have this part of you returned with a new understanding?

Take a few more moments to check in with how you feel. You might want to jot down any insights or simply let them settle in your mind, trusting that your unconscious will hold onto what's important.

Final Thoughts on Moving Toward Alignment

As we've explored, aligning your head, heart, and gut is essential to truly understanding and working with your anxiety. Each centre offers its own wisdom, and when all three are aligned, they empower you to move forward in ways that feel authentic, grounded, and true to who you are.

Much of this approach to alignment is inspired by the profound training I received from Dr. Heidi Heron and NLP Worldwide Institutes. The more I delve into this work, the more I realise that healing comes from listening to all parts of ourselves.

Now that you've started listening to each part, you're ready to keep moving forward. In the next chapter, we'll deepen this alignment and continue transforming your relationship with anxiety.

CHAPTER 15

Why Intention Matters

"You need to learn how to select your thoughts just the same way you select your clothes every day. This is a power you can cultivate."

~ Eat Pray Love Movie

As we've explored how our head, heart, and gut inform our experience of anxiety and guide our decisions, it's essential to bring awareness to the hidden intentions behind our actions. Often, our conscious mind thinks it's acting for one reason, while beneath the surface, deeper motivations—sometimes rooted in anxiety or fear—are subtly influencing us.

NLP Presupposition: Every behaviour has a positive intention. (Even the behaviours we don't like about ourselves)

Sometimes, we don't recognise our anxiety for what it is. We may believe we're being cautious, protective, or proactive, but in truth, these actions might be driven by something subtler.

Let me share an example.

My Story - *The Gap-Filler*

In recent years, through deeply effective therapy (thank you, Dr. Heidi Heron and NLP Coach Sandip Mukherjee), I realised I was a proficient "gap-filler." You may be wondering, what exactly is a gap-filler? I even felt the need to hyphenate it to fill the gap—just kidding.

For years, I instinctively filled any gap I saw, heard, or felt—especially within my family. If someone struggled to communicate, I'd step in to smooth things over. If someone didn't know how to handle something—whether it was a banking app, a loan payment, or remembering a birthday—I would jump in to take care of it. I thought I was being helpful, relieving stress, and solving problems.

And I was—but there was more to it.

I believed my intention was to support, protect, and help my loved ones. But through therapy, I uncovered a deeper motivation. I wasn't just easing their stress; I was creating a sense of safety and stability for myself. I'd been filling these gaps because, at the core, I felt a need to be indispensable. What if I didn't step in? Would I still be valuable? Would they still love me?

Uncovering Hidden Motivations

This is why understanding the true intention behind our behaviours is so crucial. Sometimes, what we think we're doing to help others is actually a way of managing our anxiety. We may believe we're preventing others from making mistakes or helping them avoid discomfort when, in reality, we're soothing our own unease.

The true intention behind our actions might not be what we initially think.

Consider moments when you step in to help others. Ask yourself:

- *For what purpose am I doing this?*

- *What is important to me about this?*

- *What do I believe would happen if I didn't step in?*

Gap-Filling: Protecting vs. Nurturing

One important distinction I've learned is the difference between protecting and nurturing. When we "fill in the gaps" for others, we often think we're protecting them from harm or discomfort. Yet, discomfort is where growth happens. If we shield others too much from challenges, we deny them the chance to learn, grow, and build resilience.

Think of a young seedling. In its early stages, we protect it in a controlled environment to shield it from harsh conditions. But as it grows, we gradually expose it to sun, wind, and rain. If we overprotect it, the seedling won't develop the strength to thrive on its own. Nurturing is about providing care while still allowing for growth and exposure to life's challenges.

The same principle applies to our relationships. When we step in to fix everything for the people we care about, we're not only protecting them from discomfort but also potentially holding them back. True nurturing allows others to face challenges, fostering their own resilience and growth.

Your True Intentions

As you reflect on your behaviours, especially in relationships, start to notice where you might be stepping in to fill the gaps for others. Are you saying yes when you really want to say no? Are you rescuing others from discomfort because you feel anxious about what might happen if you don't?

Ask yourself:

- *What is my true motivation for stepping in?*

- *What am I afraid will happen if I don't?*

- *What would change if I trusted them to handle things on their own?*

Moving from Protecting to Nurturing

When we begin to recognise our hidden motivations, we start to see the difference between protecting and nurturing. We notice when our actions are driven by anxiety and the need to fill gaps, and we understand that by stepping back, we allow others the space to grow. This awareness is where real progress begins—it's the moment we shift from protecting those around us to nurturing them.

This is where the *M* in the CALM model—move—comes into play. Once you become aware of these hidden motivations, you can start moving forward. You can shift from protecting, which often comes from your own discomfort and anxiety to nurturing, where you support others in their growth without feeling the need to shield them from every challenge. By making this shift, you relieve yourself of the constant burden of vigilance and allow your loved ones to develop their strength and resilience.

Interestingly, the word *protect* comes from the Latin *protegere*, which combines *pro-* ("in front") and *-tegere* ("to cover"). When you protect someone, you're literally standing in front of them, shielding them from harm—just like we often do when we "fill the gap" for others. But true growth doesn't happen under constant protection. When we move from protecting to nurturing, we allow others the chance to face discomfort, which fosters their growth. Bit by bit, we remove the protective cover, giving them space to develop resilience.

As you continue this journey, pay attention to those moments when your anxiety urges you to protect, and gently consider how you can shift toward nurturing instead. In making this transition, you not only support others' growth but also find a new freedom for yourself, allowing your relationships to flourish without the need for hypervigilance.

Embodiment of the Healed You

By now, you've come a long way in understanding and releasing your anxiety and stepping into the person you desire to be. In this next chapter, we focus on *embodying* the healed version of yourself. This isn't just about thinking differently—it's about integrating these changes into every aspect of your being.

Robert Dilts' Logical Levels model helps us understand that true transformation isn't just about changing our surroundings or behaviours. Real, lasting change happens when we shift at deeper levels—where our beliefs, identity, and sense of purpose reside.

Dilts' Logical Levels

Robert Dilts' model is like a staircase, with each level building upon the previous one. It begins with our environment and moves upward through our behaviours, capabilities, values, beliefs, identity, and, finally, our purpose. Let's reflect on how you can use this model to fully embody your healed self.

- **Environment:** This is the world around you, where your anxiety may have been triggered in the past. Perhaps you've changed jobs, relationships, or places, hoping it would ease your anxiety, only to find it returned. This is because true transformation requires more than just changing your surroundings.

- **Behaviours:** These are the actions you take. You may have tried to manage anxiety by altering your behaviour—avoiding triggers, saying no to social events, or trying new coping strategies. However, behaviour alone isn't enough to create lasting change.

- **Capabilities:** Your abilities and skills. Maybe you've learned techniques to manage anxiety, like mindfulness or meditation. These tools are valuable, but true transformation happens when we look deeper at why we need these skills in the first place.

- **Beliefs & Values:** These are the driving forces behind your capabilities and behaviours. Your beliefs about yourself shape how you show up. If you believe deep down, *I'm an anxious person,* no amount of behavioural changes will fully alleviate anxiety. In this journey, you've already begun to shift these beliefs. Here is where change deepens.

- **Identity:** Who you believe yourself to be. Your sense of self plays a huge role in how you experience life. If anxiety has been a part of your identity, it's time to rewrite that story. Who are you when anxiety no longer defines you?

- **Purpose/Spirituality**: This is your reason for being, your connection to something greater. When you have a strong sense of purpose, everything else aligns. What are you here for now that anxiety is no longer at the helm?

Client Story - *Embodying Your True Self*

I remember a client. Let's call her Vicki, an artist in her sixties who had given everything to her family - but now, having come out as gay later in life – she felt lost, adrift. Isolated on a remote island, she was ready to give up, believing life had become too hard. She planned to spend her last days there, feeling adrift and without purpose. Over a series of sessions, we gradually talked her back from the edge. As she opened up, she shared her dreams—her vision of rebuilding her art school and travelling the world to share her love of painting. Yet, she struggled to feel excited about these dreams; her identity was bound up in failure, loss, and regret.

Together, we explored these feelings, tracing the roots of beliefs like, *I'm a fraud. I'm alone. I'm just scraping by.* We connected to memories where these beliefs had taken hold, and she began to understand why she often chose avoidance or "all or nothing" thinking. We sat with the discomfort, revisiting some painful memories, and finally, she allowed herself to dream.

As we mapped out her dreams using Dilts' model, she imagined how her environment would change if she were living this new life. She pictured herself in a welcoming space where she could teach art classes, just like she used to. We discussed her behaviours, such as how she would show up confidently as Art Teacher Vicki, connect with students, and share her passion. Her capabilities—her creative skills—would enable her to connect with people worldwide, helping her build a meaningful life. Her beliefs—she could now embrace *I made it. I'm living my dream.* Her identity—she could see herself as Art Teacher Vicki, a successful artistic mentor, celebrating diversity, leaving behind a legacy of connection and passion for creativity. I thought of the movie *The Greatest Showman*—a place where people came together, finding joy and belonging.

Finally, her purpose—to connect with people, share her love of painting, and leave behind something meaningful—and even more important, Vicki found her answer to why all of this mattered: Vicki wanted to help other women and men coming out as gay, late in life, to navigate the feelings of loss, confusion and loneliness. She wanted people to know they were not alone and her legacy to be one of her contributions to life .. to know she mattered because she'd made a difference.

By embodying this future self, Vicki began to see that she wasn't as lost as she thought. She was standing at the edge of her potential, ready to step into the person she was meant to be.

Why Embodiment Matters

Now, it's your turn. This is where the *M* in the CALM model truly comes into play: it's time to *Move* into the healed version of yourself by fully embodying who you want to be. When you embody change, you're not just thinking differently—you're living differently. You're integrating your new beliefs and behaviours at every level of your being.

Dilts' model reminds us that changing only our environment or behaviours brings short-term results at best. But when you embody your healed self—when your identity shifts and your beliefs align with that identity—your environment and behaviours transform as natural extensions of who you've become.

Think about who you are without anxiety as a driving force. Envision how you will show up in your life now that you're free from patterns that once held you back. Visualise it. Feel it. Let this new reality take root within you.

Journal Questions to Clarify Who You Are

Use these questions to clarify and deepen your understanding of the person you're becoming:

- *Who am I now, without anxiety?*

- *What beliefs do I hold about myself now that I am free from anxiety?*

- *What values guide my decisions and actions in this new phase of my life?*

- *How am I showing up differently in my relationships, work, and daily life?*

Affirming Statements to Take with You

Carry these affirmations as reminders of your strength and newfound freedom:

- *"I am calm, grounded, and confident in who I am."*

- *"I trust my ability to navigate challenges with ease."*

- *"I am free from patterns of anxiety and step into my true self with grace."*

Acknowledging How Far You've Come

Pause for a moment to reflect on your journey through this book. You've come so far. You've explored your thoughts, emotions, and beliefs. You've listened to the wisdom of your head, heart, and gut. You've moved through difficult moments, and now, you stand at the threshold of something new—a healed version of yourself. Acknowledge this transformation and honour the courage it's taken to get here.

Embodiment Practice | Neurological Embodiment

Let's fully integrate everything you've learned with practice to embody the healed version of yourself. This exercise will guide you through each of the neurological levels.

Take a deep breath. Imagine the person you want to be—the person who is free from anxiety. Picture yourself living the life you've always desired. Make this vision vivid and clear, as bright and colourful as possible. Amplify everything you're feeling as you stand in this new version of yourself. Now, holding onto this powerful state and knowing it's closer than ever, let your mind step back through the following levels:

1. **Purpose:** Connect with your higher purpose. Why are you here? What larger mission or calling drives you now that anxiety no longer holds you back?

2. **Identity:** Who are you now? Without anxiety, how do you define yourself? What roles do you play in your life, and how do they feel different now that you're no longer weighed down by anxiety?

3. **Beliefs:** Consider what you now believe about yourself. How have your beliefs about your worth and future shifted? Write down these new beliefs that affirm your growth.

4. **Capabilities:** Reflect on the new skills and strengths you've developed. What inner resources have you gained through this journey? What are you now capable of that you weren't before?

5. **Behaviours:** Notice how you're behaving differently now. Observe the subtle changes in your daily actions. Notice how you are perhaps more relaxed, confident, or assertive. Write down how you'll show up in your relationships and interactions.

6. **Environment:** Visualise your surroundings. Notice your environment from this entirely different perspective now that you're free from anxiety. What's different about the people, places, and spaces you interact with?

As you step through each level, allow yourself to fully embody this new version of yourself. Notice how your posture changes, how your breath steadies, and how a sense of calm and clarity settles within.
156

Moving Forward

This is your new reality—one where anxiety no longer dictates your life. You are free to move forward, to create, to love, and to live fully. Let this journey become a foundation you return to whenever you need strength. Embrace the healed version of yourself with confidence, knowing that you are ready to step into the life you've envisioned.

CHAPTER 16

Sage Advice: Returning to Your Life... and Your World

"In the infinity of life where I am, all is perfect, whole, and complete. I no longer choose to believe in old limitations and lack. I now choose to begin to see myself as the Universe sees me --- perfect, whole, and complete."

~ Louise Hay

As you grow and change, the world around you will notice. Sometimes, this can create tension with those who are used to the "old" you. It's natural for people to feel unsettled when someone close to them starts setting boundaries or making different choices. But these shifts are essential—they reflect your progress and your commitment to living authentically. Let's explore a story that illustrates this journey of change and the strength it takes to stay true to yourself.

Client Story - *A Young Mother's Boundaries*

A young single mother came to me for support in setting boundaries with her family. She has four children under six and relies heavily on family members for help. Working full-time as a nurse, she often felt burned out and guilty for needing so much support. Though her family helped with the kids, they constantly complained to her about each other, leaving her feeling trapped and out of integrity. Out of gratitude, she felt obligated to engage in these negative conversations, which weighed heavily on her.

We worked through various techniques, and two weeks later, she came back, proud of the boundaries she'd put in place. Yet, her family kept saying, "You've changed." She didn't know how to respond because she didn't feel she had changed—she felt more authentic than ever. I asked, "Do you feel good about the changes you've made?" She said yes. "Then next time they say, 'You've changed,' maybe just say, 'Thank you.'"

This reaction—*You've changed*—is one many people experience as they grow and set new boundaries. While it might feel challenging, these comments reflect the impact of your growth and the adjustments others have to make. Let's look at why this is not only normal but something to embrace.

1. "What's Happened to You? You're Different."

People like familiarity—it makes them feel safe. When we act in predictable ways, others can relax because they know what to expect. But as you've been working on yourself, your behaviour naturally shifts. You make new choices, set boundaries, or say no to things that no longer serve you. This can feel unsettling for those around you, used to the "old" you. They may say things like, "You've changed."

And the truth is, you *have* changed—and that's worth celebrating.

2. You've Changed… and That's a Great Thing.

Many of my clients notice that as they make progress, some people around them feel uncomfortable or even unsupportive. I've experienced this, too. When I let go of my fear of judgment and began setting boundaries, my newfound confidence made some people uneasy.

But change isn't just inevitable—it's essential for growth. When you change how you respond, it invites others to change as well. Your relationships, interactions, and dynamics shift because you are no longer the same person. This may feel disorienting to those who haven't been part of your journey, but remember: you are stepping into a more authentic version of yourself, guided by self-awareness and calm rather than anxiety.

3. T.T.T. – Table Tennis Tiny

Personal change is like a game of table tennis. Imagine you and I are hitting the ball back and forth. As long as we keep returning it the same way, nothing changes. But if I make even the smallest adjustment—if I turn my paddle slightly—the ball takes a new direction, and you have to adjust to stay in the game.

This is how personal change works. Even a tiny shift in you can create a ripple effect, requiring those around you to respond differently. Next time you feel frustrated with someone's behaviour (or even your own), think "TTT—Table Tennis Tiny." Make one tiny change and watch the impact.

4.   As You Change, the People Around You Change.

Your change isn't isolated; it affects everyone around you. When you alter how you respond, others can no longer interact with the same version of you—they are forced to adjust, whether they want to or not.

Often, this is when you'll hear, "What's gotten into you?" or "You're different." People who have known you a long time may find your changes unsettling, sometimes resisting them. What they're truly resisting is the change they need to make within themselves to keep up with your growth.

As your anxiety fades, you'll find you no longer need to fill gaps or smooth over discomfort. Those gaps, while uncomfortable at first, are where real growth occurs. You're giving the people around you the same opportunity for growth that you've given yourself.

5.   Moving Forward: From Protecting to Nurturing

As you move forward, embrace the fact that your change will inspire change in others. Some may resist; others will grow alongside you. This is your moment to release the anxiety-driven behaviours of the past and step into a nurturing, supportive role for yourself and those around you.

You've changed—and that's powerful. When someone says, "You've changed," smile and say, "Thank you." Because you *have* changed, you've shifted from protecting yourself through anxiety to nurturing growth in yourself and those around you.

And that, my friend, is truly something to be proud of.

Embodying Your Transformation

As we come to the close of this chapter—and this book—I want to share something from my own journey of healing, as it may mirror what you're feeling now. When I first discovered Louise Hay's work, I thought, *Yes! This is it. This will fix me.* I immersed myself in her teachings, absorbing so much wisdom and feeling as though I'd found the answer I'd been searching for. And in that moment, it was.

Then I encountered the Enneagram, and once again, I thought, *Yes! This is it. This will fix me.* Through the Enneagram, I began to unravel the invisible patterns and deeply rooted beliefs holding me back. I gained a new understanding of my personality and how it connected to my anxiety, offering insights I hadn't accessed before.

And then I found NLP, and once more, I thought, *Yes! This is it. This will fix me.* NLP opened up another dimension, showing me how my mind processed anxiety and how I could rewire my thought patterns to respond with calm instead of panic.

Each of these tools—Louise Hay's teachings, the Enneagram, NLP—along with the incredible mentors I've had the honour to learn from, like Robert Bruce, Mackayla Chalmers, Heidi Heron, Laureli Blythe, Ingrid Hurwitz, have all been transformative. They offered me insights, tools, and support along my path. But here's the truth: while each of these resources and mentors is remarkable, there is no single answer, no magic pill, no final point where you are "fixed."

Because that implies there was something broken.

The reality is that you are not broken. You never were.

You are evolving and growing, and every phase of your journey will bring new people, new tools, and new insights to support your growth— just as this book, I hope, has. But this book is not "the" answer, and that's perfectly okay. Louise Hay, the Enneagram, NLP—none of these is "the" answer. They are all part of an ongoing evolution.

This is not the end.

It's the beginning—the beginning of an exciting next chapter for you, the real you, the one you're rediscovering and learning to love.

As we move into the final exercises of this book, remember: this journey doesn't end here. It is an ongoing, evolving path, and new tools and people will continue to enter your life exactly when you need them.

As Louise Hay says, "People and information come to me at the perfect time and space sequence in my life."

My First Introduction to the Enneagram

Let me share a story from my journey, one that profoundly shifted the way I saw myself and my anxiety.

I remember sitting in a humid room with expansive ceilings and exposed timber beams. The space was filled with oversized floor cushions in colours that reminded me of Thailand and ceiling fans that struggled to bring any sense of relief to the warmth and humidity. I was in Byron Bay—it was spring/summer, and need I say more? I was nervous—feeling like I didn't belong. Everyone else seemed so calm and serene. Did I mention it was Byron Bay, New South Wales, Australia? People sat around me, legs crossed on their floor cushions, eyes closed, smiling, meditative, so peaceful—everything I wasn't.

A woman with beautiful, flowing grey hair floated toward me and introduced herself as Mackayla. We chatted briefly. I don't even remember what we spoke about. But her *presence*—that I remember. Something about her both unnerved and intrigued me. It was as though she could see me, truly see me. I was filled with the urge to run, but something held me in place. I felt disoriented, like the walls of my familiar world were shifting. The structure I had held in place for so long… was shaking.

That was my first introduction to the Enneagram. It was like looking into a mirror that reflected parts of myself I had never seen before. The Enneagram helped me understand the invisible ties that had restricted me in life, and it allowed me to reconnect with qualities within myself that I hadn't even realised existed. It revealed the hidden gifts that my anxiety had been holding all along.

This book is not about the Enneagram, but I mention it here because it was an integral part of my journey. As I continued to study with Robert Bruce and Mackayla and later with Ingrid Hurwitz, delving into the intersection of the Enneagram and trauma, I began to understand that anxiety isn't the enemy. In fact, it can be a gift, a doorway into deeper wisdom, if we know how to access it.

My journey with the Enneagram is ongoing, and it will perhaps be the focus of my next book, where I'm considering sharing how to weave this ancient wisdom into your own healing journey because anxiety isn't bad. It might have *felt* bad. But I hope you know now that anxiety holds hidden wisdom. Inside our anxiety are nuggets of information that we can use. Anxiety can be a gift. When we uncover the wisdom it holds, we can wield it with grace throughout the various aspects of our lives.

After all, if anxiety had never shown up in your life, we would never have had the chance to take this beautiful journey together, and you may never have had the chance to uncover some of the hidden wisdom of your own anxiety.

Final Exercise: Dear Younger Self Therapy

Now that we've explored these powerful tools and insights, it's time to integrate everything you've learned. This exercise will help you connect with your younger self, offering them the wisdom, love, and support they may not have received at the time but which you now have in abundance. Use this as an opportunity to give back to the younger version of yourself—gifting them the understanding they need and healing those early experiences that shaped much of your anxiety.

Steps

1. **Find a Quiet Space:** Settle into a calm, comfortable space where you won't be interrupted. Close your eyes and take a few deep breaths, allowing your body to relax.

2. **Picture Your Younger Self:** Imagine yourself at a much younger age—a time when you remember feeling uncertain, anxious, or afraid. Try to picture this younger version of yourself vividly. Imagine them sitting or standing in front of you.

3. **Notice Their Emotions:** Observe the expression on their face, their body language, and any emotions they might be feeling. Recognise the innocence and vulnerability they held at that moment.

4. **Offer Words of Comfort:** Imagine reaching out to this younger self. Speak to them gently, acknowledging their fears or struggles. Let them know that they are not alone and that they have a caring, wiser version of themselves (you) supporting them now.

5. **Share Your Wisdom:** Tell them about the journey you've been on and the insights you've gained. Offer them the wisdom and tools you've learned from this book, letting them know that they have the strength within themselves to overcome their challenges.

6. **Give Reassurance:** Let your younger self know that it's okay to feel anxious and that these feelings don't define them. Reassure them that they are worthy, whole, and deserving of peace and happiness.

7. **Embrace Your Younger Self:** If it feels right, imagine embracing this younger version of yourself. Visualise warmth and love flowing between you, filling both of you with a sense of calm and connection.

8. **Return to the Present:** Gently release the image of your younger self, bringing your awareness back to the present moment. Take a few deep breaths and notice how you feel, carrying forward the compassion and strength you've shared.

9. **Reflect in Writing:** If you feel inspired, write a letter to your younger self, capturing the supportive words you shared. Let this letter be a lasting reminder of the love, wisdom, and healing you now offer to yourself.

By connecting with your younger self in this way, you're creating space for healing and self-compassion. Each time you practice this exercise, you strengthen your ability to nurture and support yourself, past and present. Remember, this journey doesn't end here—it's an ongoing path of growth and rediscovery.

Taking Back Your Life: Reprogramming for Your Future

Here you are, standing on the edge of something new. You've

done the work, dug deep, and started a powerful transformation. But remember, this isn't the end—it's just the beginning of a life where you are no longer defined by anxiety but guided by your own strength, clarity, and purpose.

The path forward doesn't have to be grand or perfect. It's about small, intentional steps and gentle choices each day that keep you connected to your real self. Set goals that feel grounded in who you are now. Give yourself the grace to take things one step at a time. Each choice you make, however small, is a reminder of the life you're creating—one where you live with peace, joy, and true presence.

Think of this as a beautiful, unfolding journey. There will be new discoveries, more tools, and, yes, a few challenges, but you're ready for all of it. You have everything you need to keep stepping forward, aligned with your heart, mind, and soul.

So here it is: It is your time to take back your life, to reprogram your future, and to walk forward with confidence. The possibilities ahead of you are endless, and they are yours to explore.

Take a deep breath. Step forward. Your life, as you've always wanted to live it, is waiting.

References

1. Australian Bureau of Statistics. "National Study of Mental Health and Wellbeing, 2020-2022." Available at: https://www.abs.gov.au/statistics/health/mental-health/national-study-mental-health-and-wellbeing/latest-release

2. Mental Health Australia. "The Cost-of-Living Crisis is Dramatically Impacting Australians' Mental Health." Available at: https://mhaustralia.org/media-releases/cost-living-crisis-dramatically-impacting-australians-mental-health

3. Cambridge University Press & Assessment. "Indirect Costs of Depression and Other Mental and Behavioural Disorders for Australia from 2015 to 2030." Available at: https://www.cambridge.org/core/journals/bjpsych-open/article/indirect-costs-of-depression-and-other-mental-and-behavioural-disorders-for-australia-from-2015-to-2030/ [DOI link]

4. Mind Medicine Australia. "Mental Health Facts." Available at: https://mindmedicineaustralia.org/mental-health-facts

Connect with the Author

Thank you for reading my book! I'd love to hear from you and stay connected. Here are several ways you can reach out and follow my work:

Follow me on social media for updates, insights, and daily musings:

- Instagram: https://www.instagram.com/tabathakattau/
- Facebook: https://www.facebook.com/tabathakattau/
- Facebook: https://www.facebook.com/sincerusmindsetcoaching/

Visit my official website for more information about my books, upcoming events, and blog posts:

www.sincerusmindsetcoaching.com

Stay up-to-date with my latest releases, writing progress, and exclusive content by subscribing to my Sunday Thoughts email list:

https://sincerusmindsetcoaching.activehosted.com/f/4

As a resident of Sedgefield, NSW, Australia, I'm always excited to connect with local readers and writers. Keep an eye out for my appearances at:

- Singleton Library
- Local book clubs
- Writers' workshops in the Newcastle and surrounding areas

I will be participating in book signings and literary events across Australia. Check my website or social media for upcoming appearances near you.

For inquiries about speaking engagements, interviews, or other professional matters, please contact me at tabatha@sincerusmindsetcoaching.com

I genuinely appreciate your support and look forward to connecting with you!

Kind thoughts,
Tabatha